For Charlie, Olivia and Florence

ZENDA

The Unauthorized Biog

ZENDAYA

The Unauthorized Biography

Alison James

Michael O'Mara Books Limited

First published in Great Britain in 2023 by
Michael O'Mara Books Limited
9 Lion Yard
Tremadoc Road
London SW4 7NQ

A CIP catalogue record for this book is available from the British Library.

Papers used by Michael O'Mara Books Limited are natural, recyclable products made from wood grown in sustainable forests. The manufacturing processes conform to the environmental regulations of the country of origin.

ISBN: 978-1-78929-548-1 in hardback print format
ISBN: 978-1-78929-551-1 in ebook format

1 2 3 4 5 6 7 8 9 10

Designed and typeset by Natasha Le Coultre and Claire Cater
Printed and bound by CPI Group (UK) Ltd, Croydon, CR0 4YY

www.mombooks.com

MIX
Paper | Supporting responsible forestry
FSC
www.fsc.org   FSC® C171272

Contents

Introduction

Once in every lifetime a star is born who shines so brightly, that person transcends all others in the firmament. Zendaya is one such supernova. She is so special that it's almost as if she is not of this world – or, indeed, this galaxy – but from another solar system altogether, one where it is a given that celestial beings are blessed with multiple gifts and great beauty. If Zendaya had possessed only one talent, she would still have risen to the top, but it seems there is nothing this native California girl cannot do. Her acting ability has led to her winning countless awards, including two prestigious Emmys and a Golden Globe, her debut album went platinum and when she dances it's impossible to take your eyes off her. But that's not all: Zendaya is fearless where all things regarding fashion are concerned. If she was to dress in a shapeless sack cloth, it is likely it would become the next big sartorial trend. She instantly makes every red carpet she walks her own: she is queen of the red carpet, reigning supreme in exquisite designer gowns that she wears with such flair, style and panache, it is as if she was born to do it.

In reality, nothing could be further from the truth. Zendaya Maree Stoermer Coleman was not born into privilege or riches. She is the only child of a union between an African-American father and a California-born mother with Scottish and German roots, and both her parents were teachers who worked hard to earn every penny. They were not able to lavish Zendaya with material wealth, but what they did bestow on her was far more valuable. They imbued in her a strong sense of self-belief, as well as supporting her talents, extraordinary confidence and her ability to love herself – although never in a narcissistic or self-obsessed way. They also passed down humility, down-to-earth sensibilities, a conscientious work ethic, gratitude and the courage to speak out for what she believed to be right and true.

As a girl growing up with a mixed-race heritage, Zendaya experienced systemic racism first-hand. Regardless, she was determined to push open doors in order to let her light shine through as brightly as it should – and once opened, she has been just as determined to hold these doors ajar for those who come after her. She is as passionate about this mission as she is about her career – a career which, in effect, started as soon as she had her light bulb moment as a small child. Filaments in her brain sparked away as she spent hours watching actors onstage at the Shakespearean theatre where her mother Claire also worked. They would spark again when she watched Miley Cyrus as Hannah Montana on television. Zendaya wanted to be Hannah so badly, she would often cry while watching her favourite show. But could it, would it ever happen to a little girl of mixed ethnicity like her? Through her talent, hard work, dedication and a determination that belied her tender years, she *did* make it happen. However, it also meant personal sacrifice and living apart from her much-loved mother while she and her father, at her own suggestion, moved south to Hollywood in pursuit of her dream. She was just thirteen years old when she was cast as Rocky Blue in Disney Channel's *Shake It Up.* She had made her dream come true, and in the years that followed she went on to make many more a reality – and not just for herself. Zendaya was thinking predominantly of her fans, followers and the little girls like the one she had once been when, at just seventeen years old, she refused to become involved in her second Disney television project unless they made significant changes. As far as she was concerned, featuring a family of colour on the show was a no-brainer. Executives had no choice but to concur – if they had refused, they would have lost her. Despite her success, she still had to respond to a casually racist comment about wearing her hair in 'locs' at the Oscars. At just eighteen years old, Zendaya responded with such grace, maturity and rationale, America – and the world – sat up and took notice. This girl was special. Very special.

With an intelligence and wisdom way beyond her years, coupled with a unique fashion sense and a genius partnership with image architect Law Roach, Zendaya made the transition from Disney kid to film star with great style and success, and she did this while maintaining her innate integrity and sense of social justice. With such a wise head on young shoulders, Zendaya's maturity and measured way of viewing the world astounds all who meet her. The great and the good of the film, television and fashion industries are in awe of her talent, her uniquely charming chutzpah, her fearlessness when it comes to taking on new projects, and her incomparable style. They also praise her humility and lack of A-lister ego – she is no 'don't-you-know-who-I-am?' diva. Zendaya is, at heart, a woman of the people, especially her own people. She has never forgotten her roots or where she comes from, and she never will. These qualities are perhaps why so many people regard her as an inspiration and a role model. At a last count, her Instagram followers numbered a staggering 165 million – more than half the population of the USA – and this figure is growing all the time. Zendaya is very aware of the enormous responsibility that comes with this platform, and she cuts her cloth accordingly. Little wonder then that she was on the 2022 list of *TIME* magazine's one hundred most influential people in the world. She is also half of one of the most famous real-life couples in the world. Her romance with her *Spider-Man* co-star, Tom Holland, almost broke the internet when, after years of speculation, it finally came to light in summer 2021. 'Tomdaya', as they are singularly known, regularly tops the polls as Hollywood's cutest couple.

It is incredible to think that Zendaya is still only in her mid-twenties, so she is not even close to reaching her prime. It's tempting to project forward to try to predict how her future will pan out, but hold that thought for now – First, let this book take you right back to the beginning of Zendaya's extraordinary journey, from painfully shy little girl to the brightest star on the planet.

ONE

Daydream Believer

'I was that weird eight year old who was really interested in Shakespeare and understood it and appreciated the language' – **Zendaya**

For most seven-year-old girls, having to tag along with their mother while she worked a second job at a local theatre group would have been one big bore, in fact, a total yawn-fest. But then Zendaya Coleman wasn't most seven year olds. Since turning two, she had spent much of her childhood at the California Shakespeare Theater in Orinda, near San Francisco, which her mother managed when not working as a teacher. For this young girl with the shyest of smiles, sitting in the empty auditorium and watching the actors rehearse up on stage was an electric experience. It started as a kind of slow-burn, dimly glowing light bulb moment that gradually became brighter and brighter until it illuminated absolutely everything in her orbit. Zendaya couldn't remember a time when she hadn't been mesmerized.

'Even as a little girl I had big dreams,' she would later write in her 2013 tween self-help book *Between U and Me: How to Rock Your Tween Years with Style and Confidence*. 'I knew I wanted to be an entertainer. I could see myself singing and dancing in front of millions of people. I just knew that any dream was within my reach if I believed in myself. Achievers are also great dreamers.'

Young Zendaya was predicting her own destiny. By the time she was thirteen years old, her dream was well on the way to becoming reality.

The bay-side city of Oakland in northern California is known as San Francisco's sunnier neighbour. It is a diverse metropolis bursting with creativity and local pride: art is everywhere in Oakland, from museums and galleries to more than a thousand murals adorning the city's streets. It is also where, fittingly enough, Zendaya Maree Stoermer Coleman first made her entrance into the world at approximately six o'clock in the evening on Sunday, 1 September 1996, a baby girl born under the star sign of Virgo. It had been a difficult sixteen-hour labour for her mother, Claire Stoermer, then aged thirty-two, and a tough birth. The baby had a large head and weighed in at a hefty ten pounds. Zendaya's unique first name was inspired by the word *Tendai*, meaning 'to express gratefulness' in the Shona language, a Bantu dialect native to the people of Zimbabwe in southern Africa, where her father's ancestors are from.

'My name means "to give thanks" in Shona, and it was actually kind of half made up and half real,' Zendaya was later to reveal to *Popstar* magazine in 2011. She also explained in an interview with *The Hollywood Reporter* in the same year that the original plan was to give her a name beginning with J, but her father had the idea to add the letter Z to the start of her name instead. 'It started off [as] Jendaya, or something like that, and my dad has a thing for Z's and zen, very nice and calm, and so ... he helped name me Zendaya.'

Born Samuel David Coleman in Arkansas, USA, in February 1960, Zendaya's African-American dad changed his name to Kazembe Ajamu Coleman in homage to his ancestry. He also has Icelandic and Macedonian blood running through his veins, inherited from his father's side of the gene pool. Zendaya's mother, Claire Marie Stoermer, born in March 1964, is of German and Scottish descent. Claire's maternal grandfather, Douglas Whitelaw, left the Scottish city of Dundee at just fifteen years old to emigrate to Canada in 1911. He arrived first in Halifax and then took a train to Vancouver, where his father had already set up a business as a certified public accountant. Douglas went on to marry a Canadian girl, Thelma Ray Kelly, and their baby girl – Zendaya's future maternal grandmother, Daphne Carol – was born in Vancouver in 1939. In her late teens, Daphne went to college in California and it's here she met Claire's father, Philip, a fifth-generation Californian whose family had emigrated from Germany in the nineteenth century. Philip was a lawyer who also took photographs – his father, Fritz, was a celebrated snapper during the golden age of Hollywood.

'My mother's proud of where she's from, and her history, and her past, and same with my dad,' Zendaya said in a video celebrating Immigrant Heritage Month in 2015. 'I have roots in Africa. Like, I am from Africa as well as from Germany and Scotland, and I am very proud of that. I am a mixture of both worlds.'

This could be something of a double-edged sword, as Zendaya would begin to realize as she grew up.

'You get the best and the worst of both worlds,' she told Complex website in 2015. 'I know there were a lot of times when you try to figure out where you fit in. I just realized that it worked to my advantage because I just got along with a lot of people. But to literally be two races, it's really hard to see color because I'm the gray area. I had to learn about both sides of myself and be really proud of and educated in both.'

But all this would be in the future. Zendaya was two years old when her parents married and she would be their only child. However, she had five half-siblings on her father's side. They were considerably older than Zendaya (or 'Daya', as she was affectionately known within the family), but her three sisters, Kaylee, Katianna and Annabelle, and two brothers, Austin and Julien, formed a tight family unit around their little sister. She also had ready-made playmates in the nephews and nieces who were actually older than her. One of her nieces, Enzenia (or 'Zink' as she was known), was just a year older than Zendaya and would become particularly close to her young 'Auntie Daya'. Years later, Zendaya was quoted as saying that Zink was 'the closest person' to her.

The Stoermer/Coleman household, although not poor, was far from wealthy. Both Claire and Kazembe were educators. Claire taught at tough inner-city schools, introducing her often-disadvantaged pupils to the arts, while Kazembe was a PE teacher. Zendaya enjoyed a very happy childhood and spent a lot of time with both grandmothers. However, as a child, Zendaya was surprisingly quiet and shy – so painfully timid, in fact, that she barely spoke during her first year at kindergarten. Claire has recalled that her little daughter would sit in a circle with other children and not say a word. Claire and Kazembe were so concerned by this that they had Zendaya repeat kindergarten in the hope that she would catch up socially and emerge from her shell. They also considered which extra-curricular activities might help her to blossom. First up was basketball. Kazembe coached the sport at Emeryville High School in Oakland and Claire, standing at a statuesque 6 feet 4 inches (193 cm), had been a star hoop-shooter while studying for her Bachelor's degree at the prestigious Santa Clara University in California. Kazembe lost no time in introducing his five year old to basketball – he had lofty ambitions for her to become a member of the National Basketball Association (NBA). While there was nothing in the NBA rulebook that disallowed women and girls from joining the organization, it had never happened before. Despite Kazembe's best efforts, neither would it with Zendaya! Although she showed promise on the court, her interest in the sport began to wane after a short while.

Next up, Claire introduced her daughter to athletics, her own sport of choice. Zendaya proved to be a fast runner but, as with basketball, she soon lost interest. After a single season on the track, she hung up her tiny spikes. Sports had failed to capture her imagination, but that's not to say that nothing had. Quite the reverse, in fact. At six years old, she already knew which route she wanted to take. The 'artsy one', as she was to later tell *Essence* magazine. The signs had always been there. Her maternal grandparents had taken her to have her 'colours' read when she was just two years old, revealing that her aura was mostly purple, which is known as the creative hue, along with shades of business-like green. It was an accurate premonition. Zendaya wanted to play make-believe on the stage. She wanted to act. In addition to being mesmerized by the actors at the California Shakespeare Theater, known locally as Cal Shakes, she was also hooked on the smash-hit Disney television show *That's So Raven* and dreamed of one day starring in her own Disney series. *Hannah Montana* also had a massive impact, with Zendaya later recalling in an interview with PopSugar that she'd been instantly obsessed with the Miley Cyrus-starring franchise, to such an extent that she would cry when watching the show because she so wanted to be on television playing Hannah. Although still shy in public, Zendaya was forever singing, dancing and playing 'let's pretend' when she was at home, and both Kazembe and Claire had an instinctive feeling that their girl had something special, that elusive 'X' factor. If only she could be persuaded to show the world! Finally, Kazembe talked Zendaya into singing a duet with him at a concert at Oakland's

Redwood Day School, where he was teaching at the time. Her performance brought the house down.

'Her little, teeny voice just cut through that big giant room and, right then, I knew she had it,' Kazembe was to recall in an interview with the California-based local newspaper *Mercury News*.

For Zendaya, it was an equally memorable occasion.

'My dad was like … "I want you to try it and see if you like it",' she told *Mercury News*. 'And then, of course, my parents were right. I got on stage, and I was ecstatic.'

At Fruitvale Elementary School, which she attended and where her mother taught, Zendaya was also developing her acting skills in addition to showing the beginnings of a social conscience. She and two close friends persuaded the school principal to put on a play celebrating Black History Month. The play went ahead with Zendaya portraying Bessie Coleman, the early American civil aviator who was the first African-American woman and first Native American to hold a pilot license. Meanwhile, in every spare moment she had, Zendaya was hanging out at Cal Shakes. She handed out programmes and sold raffle tickets, but it was the creative process that fascinated her, and she absorbed the atmosphere like a sponge.

'Technical rehearsals can be pretty boring, but Zendaya would beg me to bring her,' Claire told Beyoncé's mother Tina Knowles-Lawson on the podcast *Talks with Mama Tina*. 'She would sit with the lady who was "on book" and hold the flashlight. Zendaya had a professional perspective on theatre and Shakespeare from a very young age.'

Claire was right. Zendaya was totally, utterly gripped by

everything Cal Shakes. She would spend her days at the theatre watching the skeleton of the tech rehearsals, then the dress rehearsals and finally the actual performances. She was fascinated by seeing how a production came together in a step-by-step process. How it would evolve from script form into a living, breathing entity with a life, character and spirit of its own. No two performances were ever the same. Each one had its own energy and magic. More than anything, Zendaya wanted to be up on stage and creating her own theatrical alchemy with people who were just as passionate about acting as she was. She was still quite young and didn't really understand why she had become so enraptured with classical theatre. Yet she had morphed into a highly unusual eight year old who had fallen in love with Shakespeare. 'I was that weird eight year old who was really interested in Shakespeare and understood it and appreciated the language,' she would later tell the *South China Morning Post*.

The staff at Cal Shakes could see how much it all meant to Zendaya and they fell in love with her for it. On show nights they would make sure she had everything she needed, providing her with a veggie burrito, chocolate chip cookie and fruit juice so that she was fed and watered, and could then sit in the back of the auditorium and absorb the plays and performances over and over and over again until she knew practically every line, every inference, every beat and movement by heart.

Once in third grade and by now attending the Redwood Day School where her father taught, Zendaya was encouraged by Claire to start attending formal, extra-curricular theatre classes at Cal Shakes.

'I had to push her to go to it,' Claire Stoermer told *Datebook*, an arts and entertainment guide for the San Francisco area. 'But I do remember seeing her up there on that stage, and just the few little moments that she had her spotlight, it was like, "whoa".'

Cal Shakes – which describes its vision as one that 'redefines classical theater for the 21st century' – enabled Zendaya to explore her calling, to refine her talent and hone her craft. Trish Tillman, a former teaching artist there, remembers working with Zendaya on scenes from Shakespeare plays, including *Macbeth* in which she played one of the three witches. But she explains it took a while for Zendaya's star quality to start shining through.

'I'd love to say she was an extraordinary, completely gifted child, but there was nothing out of the ordinary about her to begin with,' Tillman says of those early days. 'She was just getting used to what the idea of drama was and being onstage with other kids.'

It was by being put through her paces by Trish Tillman and other Cal Shakes teachers while also observing her fellow actors in the rehearsal room and onstage that Zendaya's talent was able to come to the fore. She was taught how to understand the texts, the people she was acting with, and how to harness and hone her natural qualities and artistic tendencies. Claire and Kazembe loved the effect Cal Shakes was having on their daughter (which they had witnessed it doing for many other young people). By focusing on the process, not the product, with teaching staff breaking everything down and having the students ask themselves questions like, 'What would you do if you were in this situation?', it was building her self-confidence and self-esteem, and really bringing her out of her shell.

By the time Zendaya was eleven years old and a sixth grader, Tillman started to see something special in her – 'some kind of spirit'. She cast Zendaya as Lady Anne in the *Richard III* scene where the noblewoman goes from loathing the title character to agreeing to become his wife. She carried off the role with aplomb – as she was later to do playing Celia in *As You Like It*.

Zendaya was an A student in most subjects at school but when it was time to select a middle school, Claire and Kazembe decided their daughter would thrive at a specialist school, one where her creativity as a performer would be nurtured, where her potential might be recognized and hopefully realized. There was perhaps also an additional reason why they decided to go down this route: in fifth grade, Zendaya was bullied at school.

'It can get ugly between us girls,' she wrote in *Between U and Me*. 'In my fifth grade, there was a lot of talking behind each other's backs.'

She was also becoming more racially aware: 'One day, I came to school with my hair straightened, and that was the only day anyone ever complimented me on my hair,' she told *Cosmopolitan*. 'That kind of messes with you'.

Speaking to *Glamour* magazine some years later, Zendaya recalled another incident in the fifth grade. She hadn't acted to stop a classmate from being bullied, and she revealed how ashamed it had made her feel – especially as her parents had called her out on it. From that day forward, she vowed to make it her mission to step in and advocate for bullied children whenever she could.

Aged eleven, Zendaya enrolled at Oakland School for the Arts (OSA). Initially, she was overcome with shyness. In fact, it was like she was a little girl again and all her former insecurities had come flooding back. She didn't know anyone and felt intimidated by the other students, especially the older ones. There was so much to learn and remember on a purely practical level – following a strict timetable, being in the right place at the right time, constant worries about being late for class, making friends and even figuring out how to open her locker! At elementary school as a sixth grader, she had been top dog, but now at OSA she was having to start at the bottom again in the first year. Neither could she disappear into the background while she familiarized herself with her new routine and surroundings. Oakland was a performing arts school. She was there to perform, to act, to stand up in front of her peers and teachers and let her inhibitions go as she attempted to get inside the skin of different characters. She was determined to attain good grades, to succeed and to fulfil her dreams. To achieve this, Zendaya reached deep down inside herself, plucked up her courage, stood up in front of her classmates and gave everything she had. The first time was terrifying, but the more she did it, the easier it became and soon it would become like second nature to her. Success took a while in coming, though. It is interesting to note that Zendaya's first role was not a starring one. She auditioned for one of the lead parts in Roald Dahl's *James and the Giant Peach* but ended up cast as the silkworm.

'I didn't have any lines, but you know what?' she recalled in an interview with *W* magazine, 'I killed it! I was a worm, but I was reacting and giving face, and I was the best dang silkworm there ever was.'

In retrospect, Zendaya is grateful she wasn't initially regarded as star material. In the early days at OSA, she was 'just getting used to what the idea of drama was'. In short, the school provided her with the experience she needed, and it gave her the space and training required to kick-start her acting career. As time went on and she became more confident and came out of her shell, she began to be cast for bigger roles such as the character of Ti Moune in the musical *Once on This Island* at the Berkeley Playhouse. She also played the male character Joe in the musical *Caroline, or Change* at Theaterworks in Palo Alto, California.

'A lot of creative magic happened for me at OSA,' she said in an interview on the Disney Channel. 'It was a good time for me to break out of my shell.'

Kazembe and Claire were delighted with their daughter's growing self-confidence. 'One of the things she got from it was being in a class of kids, doing these exercises and working together,' recalled Claire in a later interview on the Disney Channel.

Once she had recovered from her initial shyness at OSA, Zendaya was driven and uber-focused. 'She was disciplined at an early age, fun, hard-working,' said one of her drama tutors in the same Disney Channel interview. 'She had the kind of spirit that made everyone want to be around her.'

It wasn't just in acting that Zendaya was beginning to excel. She was also a naturally gifted dancer. She had always loved to dance around the house with her siblings and parents, and she had started 'dancing dancing' – as she called it when she joined Future Shock, an Oakland hip-hop dance troupe, at aged eight. She would later say that this was how her dance life formally started. It was tough going at first. The other kids in the group were older than her and had far more experience of hip-hop, and she found herself lagging behind. 'I wasn't very good,' she recollected in *Between U and Me*. 'I had a hard time keeping up and learning the dance moves with all the older kids, but I slowly got better and better.'

In a somewhat random move, Zendaya also spent two years training as a hula dancer with the Academy of Hawaiian Arts. She enjoyed it, but it was hip-hop rather than hula that she considered to be her strong suit. One dancer who was an important inspiration, whose iconic spins she greatly admired, was Michael Jackson. Zendaya was twelve years old when he passed away on 25 June 2009, and in homage to her hero she began watching on repeat *Michael Jackson's This Is It*, the documentary film about the rehearsals and preparation for the concert series of the same name which had been cancelled just eighteen days before his death. She also showed her devotion by dressing like Jackson for a time – favouring black skinny jeans, loafer shoes and a military-style jacket. She did, however, draw the line at glittery socks.

After a year at OSA, Zendaya's thoughts and ambitions were turning to television. Her dream of starring in a Disney show was still at the forefront of her mind. She started going for castings for commercials and modelling assignments, with Claire driving her to callbacks and auditions in the Oakland area. But Oakland wasn't exactly television central. Los Angeles – some 371 miles and six hours south – was where she needed to be. Zendaya and her father began to spend long hours traversing Interstate 5 between Oakland and LA so the adolescent could participate in auditions for commercials and other projects. However, it was neither practical nor sustainable. Eventually, something had to give. The twelve year old strongly felt she needed to be based in Hollywood to be able to further her career and fulfil her dreams. Fortunately, her ever-supportive parents agreed and Kazembe and Zendaya relocated to LA.

'I'd started going to auditions with my father,' she told the British newspaper the *Daily Mirror*. 'He quit his teaching job to accompany me to Los Angeles whenever necessary and that was a significant financial burden. As you know, teaching is one of the most important but least paid and least appreciated professions.'

Claire had always gone above and beyond what was strictly required as a teacher at an underfunded, inner-city school. She was constantly working to open her students' eyes to an education that could lift them far beyond their current circumstances. She would introduce them to the arts, guide them through the language of Shakespeare, and show them the wonders of nature outside city life – all things that they wouldn't have experienced otherwise. Watching Claire at work instilled within Zendaya a true appreciation of and devotion to the importance of education.

Claire remained in Oakland, continuing to work two jobs in order to keep the family afloat financially, while Kazembe rented a small apartment in downtown Los Angeles where he and Zendaya based themselves. Being without her mother was tough for the ambitious tween, even though she did go home to Oakland every other week. Zendaya celebrated her birthday soon after relocating and, realizing that she was missing her mother, Kazembe surprised her by flying Claire to LA for a few days. Zendaya was beside herself with joy to see her mother and equally delighted with her father for being so thoughtful and considerate of her feelings.

'I was really happy and really touched that my father was so tuned into my feelings,' she was later to remark in *Between U and Me*. 'He just knew what I wanted more than anything in the world. I missed a lot of fun things while I was pursuing my dreams and it was difficult not being able to be with my mom and my dog.'

Enrolling at a new school, Oak Park High, in a suburb of Los Angeles, didn't come easy. Oakland and Los Angeles are both in California but they are different worlds as far as Zendaya was concerned. Her shyness kicked in at finding herself the new girl again. It was tough not knowing anyone and being in a strange, new place. It took her a while to find friends. 'The change was hard for me,' she told HuffPost.

As always, Zendaya had the unswerving support of her loving parents, something she has never failed to be grateful for. She knew she owed them big-time for the sacrifices they were making to enable her to chase after her dream. Claire and Kazembe were always on board with her and right from the start had her best interests at heart. Open and honest, they involved her in all decision-making and were 100 per cent supportive of whatever she wanted to do. They were never the type to be pushy 'showbiz' parents and allowed Zendaya to call the shots.

'I always heard those tragic stories of successful young actors whose lives fall apart in later years,' she told the *Daily Mirror*, 'but my parents gave me a very good education in life and everything else. It was the best kind of upbringing that you can have.'

Zendaya was fortunate in that, with her half-siblings grown up and living their own lives, her parents were able to concentrate on her. Kazembe later told Katch Up Kulture that his youngest child had 'only child' syndrome in the most positive way possible and that, to all effects, she was raised as such. Kazembe and Claire instilled in their girl a remarkable confidence and sense of self – particularly in one so young.

'Everything starts at home and with upbringing,' Kazembe later remarked in an interview with presenter Kalima Kam on Katch Up Kulture. 'She's always known who she is. Zendaya has had the best of both worlds. On her mother's side, she comes from an upper-middle-class family, and I suppose I would consider ourselves to be middle-class, hard-working Blacks. Zendaya has learned from both sides because she learned how to navigate.'

Very true. As a child, Zendaya spent hours with her paternal grandmother, who was originally from Little Rock, Arkansas, in the American Deep South. She had met Zendaya's grandfather when she was very young and married him at just fourteen or fifteen years old. While young Zendaya would have absorbed some of her grandma's stories almost by osmosis, she later said that as she grew older, she loved nothing more than asking Kazembe's mother questions about the life she'd lived, her many siblings and what conditions had been like for Black people in the then still deeply racist Deep South of the 1940s, 50s and 60s. Conversely, the young Zendaya had also seen much of her mother Claire's family, in particular Claire's mother, Daphne, who had been raised in a prosperous home in Vancouver, Canada. There were also considerable periods of time spent with her parents at their respective schools – the inner-city one where Claire worked and Kazembe's private one, situated in a wealthy Jewish community in Oakland. The combination of these experiences meant that young Zendaya was able to witness life from many perspectives.

Sacrifices were made by all, but the move to LA paid off. Zendaya landed modelling jobs for Macy's, Mervyns and Old Navy. She was featured in an *iCarly* toys advertisement and appeared as a back-up dancer in a Sears commercial featuring Disney star Selena Gomez. It was during the filming of the Sears commercial that Zendaya, for one of the only times in her life, behaved in a diva-like fashion. According to her father in an interview with *Vogue*, she had not been happy with her performance and wanted to repeat it – if necessary, more than once. Already her perfectionist tendencies were coming into play. 'Dad, I can't go home a failure! I can't not do this!' Kazembe's reply? 'We are going home!' By all accounts, the 'going home' threat was always his go-to response whenever he was annoyed at her. That and calling her by her middle name, Maree!

'That was such a funny commercial because it's so weird to think that later on [future *Shake It Up* co-stars] Ross Lynch was in it and Leo Howard was also in it', Zendaya later told *J-14* magazine. 'And we were backup dancers, we weren't even the lead kids. It's funny where things evolved from and it's cool to start small.'

She was also a featured performer in the Kidz Bop music video for their cover of Katy Perry's 'Hot N Cold', which was released on *Kidz Bop 15* in February 2009. But she didn't land every job she went for: there were many roles she didn't get, many auditions she failed to secure. She went after so many jobs, she would later say that she lost count of them. But she always believed that persistence would pay off and her dream of becoming a performer would come true. And within months it was starting to. The people who mattered were beginning to notice Zendaya – in particular, Judy Taylor, who was vice president of casting and talent relations for the Disney Channel. For Judy, Zendaya stood out from the other kids doing the rounds of auditions. 'You never tire of watching her,' Judy later remarked.

When Disney began to put together a new drama series about teen dancers, Judy Taylor remembered one girl in particular – a certain Zendaya Maree Stoermer Coleman.

It's All in the Stars!

Zendaya's star sign is the sixth astrological sign of the zodiac: Virgo. The sun transits this area between 23 August and 22 September each year. Virgo is an earth sign, historically represented by the goddess of wheat and agriculture, an association that speaks to Virgo's deep-rooted presence in the material world. Also known as their 'sun sign', in astrological speak, an individual's star sign is about their identity. It is the essence that a person shines out into the world. It represents the vital force that drives them to seek the highest expression of their true selves. Your star or sun sign is how you answer the question 'I am', how you experience life and express your individuality. Virgos are said to be logical, hard-working, practical, perfectionist and systematic in their approach to life. Remind you of anyone?

Zendaya is a firm believer in her astrological identity, telling *Vogue Australia*, 'I do it best when I do it myself. I'm a Virgo and I know what I like.' Even as a baby, Zendaya displayed distinctly Virgoan sensibilities. Like all earth sign nippers, Virgo babies are said to be practical, calm and constantly analysing their surroundings. They also know exactly what they like and what they don't, and they will likely tell you as much as soon as they can. As she grew older, Zendaya began to exhibit even more typical qualities attributed to her star sign. Virgo children are known to often be reserved, just as Zendaya was. Their parents may worry, just as Kazembe and Claire did, because their child seems overly shy. However, this is said to be just a Virgo child's natural reserve causing them to be slow to warm up to strangers and cautious when making friends. Virgo children are not necessarily shy; rather, they're modest, quiet and focused, and they spend time listening, observing and figuring things out. They prefer to stand back and think about a situation rather than throwing themselves into it. This was certainly true of the young Zendaya. Once she had worked out that she wanted to be a performer, she started to blossom, utilizing her innate Virgoan traits to decide just what she wanted and how – with parental guidance – to go about it.

Virgo kids are really hard working as a whole, often putting a lot of pressure on themselves because they're continually striving for perfection. Sound familiar? Astrologers believe that parents can grow their Virgo child's self-esteem and confidence if they understand, validate and support what makes their Virgo child so special. Certainly, Kazembe and Claire did this without stinting.

Zendaya always strived to be a straight-A student. Not surprising. She's a Virgo! Ruled by the planet Mercury, a Virgo child has a need for constant mental stimulation and asks endless questions. They adore learning and the questions they pose are well-grounded in reality. A Virgo child is usually one of the brainiest kids in class. The one who loves finding solutions to challenging problems and makes sure things are 'just right'. They will consider all possible angles before making a decision. The Virgo child approaches each learning experience with seriousness – they want to know the 'why' and 'how' of everything, and parents should be prepared to provide detailed explanations. Virgo kids will not be fobbed off. Being educators, Claire and Kazembe fulfilled this role without question.

Even as youngsters, Virgos are sensible, logical, practical and systematic in their approach to life. And Virgoan girls, in particular, are well known for being working hard and throwing themselves 100 per cent into projects. They settle for nothing less than perfection. They are hard-working types who have a clear vision of their future and are determined to forge their own path. Virgos are constantly striving for a goal and a certain level of precision. They are single-minded perfectionists who plan for the future and will fully dedicate themselves to reach their goals and dreams. When a Virgo girl decides that she'll make something happen, watch out – because her level of self-discipline and determination will, as Zendaya has proved, be unmatched. Once Zendaya knew what she wanted to do in life, she was determined to achieve it no matter what, regardless of how much work and single-minded dedication it took. Her mission has always been to get the job done to its optimum or not do it at all. She was born to be the best, and failure is not an option. But these perfectionistic tendencies also mean Virgos often overwork themselves, so they need to carve out time to relax – even when, like Zendaya, they prefer working hard to chilling out. They have a keen eye for detail and can break down a problem into manageable parts. However, despite being high flyers, Virgos are modest and humble about their achievements, which is another typical 'Z' trait.

When it comes to creativity, Zendaya has again always ticked the right Virgo boxes. Virgo girls are typically very creative and express themselves through the arts. They love to apply their creativity when solving problems and often let their imaginations run wild. Creativity drives this astrological sign's emotional side, and they'll throw themselves into creative activities as much as their other passions.

Zendaya has said in interviews that she is not a good liar and never has been. It's unlikely she would ever have been, considering that Virgos are one of the most honest, loyal and trustworthy signs in the zodiac. When it comes to family matters, Zendaya is yet again Virgo personified. Family matters more than anything to this star sign – and Kazembe, Claire, the grandmothers, siblings, nephews, nieces and cousins are everything to Zendaya. Friends and family members often turn to Virgos in times of need because they seem wise beyond their years. Uncanny. Even as a child Zendaya was regarded as an old soul who had definitely been here before.

TWO

Shaking It Up ... and Swagging It Out!

'When I went in as Rocky, I really felt the chemistry' – **Zendaya's recollections of her *Shake It* Up audition**

Keen to replicate the success of Zendaya's dream television character Hannah Montana, by 2008 Disney's focus was on producing another smash hit teen show, putting into practice that old television-makers' adage of conjuring up something that was 'the same but different'. Veteran television producers Chris Thompson and Rob Lotterstein were assigned to the task and began developing the concept of a 'teenage female best buddy' production, a comedy series with a dance-driven aspect. With a working title of *Dance Dance Chicago*, then-president of Disney Entertainment Gary Marsh announced that 'while buddy comedies have been around since the start of television ... this is the first time anyone has incorporated dancing into the underlying premise of a sitcom.'

Two female leads would anchor the show: the main character of CeCelia or CeCe Jones, a likeable, street-smart, slightly rebellious girl, who dances in a fictional teen TV dance show in Chicago and dreams of becoming a world-famous entertainer, and CeCe's 'good girl' best friend Raquel 'Rocky' Blue, who lives in the apartment upstairs. Like CeCe, Rocky has ambitions to make it as a dancer. The series would also depict the adventures and exploits of the two besties: their life as dancers, their social life at school and the typical teenage problems they encounter at home.

Zendaya, now thirteen, was signed to Mitchell Gossett, the same agent who had discovered Miley Cyrus. He had already suggested that, like Madonna, Rihanna and Beyoncé, she should be known by only her first name, and she was more than happy to comply. Even at such a tender age, Zendaya was aware of the advantages of such a move. Although infinitely proud of her Coleman surname and the heritage that came with it, she instinctively knew that being known by just her distinctive and highly unusual first name meant she would stand out and people would remember her. Gossett put her forward for the lead role of CeCe. As a naturally talented dancer with many years of experience behind her in addition to being an accomplished actor, he hoped Zendaya would be a shoo-in for the part. However, auditioning was an arduous, drawn-out process. Up against more than two hundred other hopefuls, the selection began with an initial audition, in which Zendaya performed the Michael Jackson hit 'Leave Me Alone'. Making it through the first cut, she went on to have a second audition – known as the 'producer session' – followed by a mix-and-match with other girls. It was during this session that the producers and casting directors had a change of heart. Having seen Zendaya 'do' CeCe, they asked her to switch roles and play Rocky. Other wannabe Disney stars-in-waiting may well have quaked at the prospect of this sudden turn – or at least requested another audition time so that they could make sufficient preparations. But already the professional, Zendaya was more than up for the challenge.

'I was like, "OK – sure, I'll read for that". I was open to it,' she wrote in *Between U and Me*. 'I was willing to give it a shot. I went out to the car, studied my lines for 20 minutes, and came back and read for Rocky. I'm so glad I did. When I went in as Rocky, I really felt the chemistry. I was kicking ass! I knew what I wanted. I think they saw that.'

A young film actress from Florida called Bella Thorne was cast as CeCe, despite never having really danced before. Zendaya had seen Bella around at various other auditions, but they'd never spoken. There was one job in particular that Zendaya remembered her from, which had occurred about six months earlier. Both she and this girl had been put forward for a print advertisement and Bella had literally whirled and twirled into the audition room, brimming over with a certain edgy energy. Zendaya had wondered who she was – this girl was so full of spark and confidence. Zendaya recognized 'the twirl girl' as soon as she arrived at the Disney studios for the new show. There were many others present who had sent in tapes and auditioned but, having seen the two girls perform, the producers and casting directors narrowed it down to Zendaya and Bella. They were paired to act opposite each other and to riff off each other. There was instant chemistry between the girls. It was immediate for all to see. Zendaya blew a line, but it didn't matter as the connection, the alchemy between them, was so, so good. These two would groove along together perfectly and set televisions across the country, maybe even the world, on fire! Zendaya and Bella were the dream combo for the new show. Commenting on the casting of the two, Judy Taylor, senior vice president at the Disney Channel, commented that Zendaya was 'completely engaging' with a 'great presence' while Bella had 'high energy' and viewers would 'want to get to know her better the instant they met her'.

Zendaya was beyond happy to have finally landed a leading role in a Disney TV show. She had instinctively known that if she kept working hard and focusing on what she wanted, it would eventually happen. Following her dreams was never going to be easy – she had realized that from the earliest days. It would take hard work, never-ending dedication, a laser-like focus, endless energy, drive … and sacrifice. She missed her mother, she missed her sisters and brothers, her nephews and nieces, she missed the family dog, a giant black schnauzer named Midnight who had been in her life since she was eight years old. But stick to your vision, stick to your gut instinct and follow your dreams was Zendaya's mantra in life.

In May 2010, with the title change revealed as *Shake It Up*, the production for the show was announced to begin that July and anticipated for an autumn 2010 premiere. The more Zendaya got to know Rocky, the more 'at one' with the character she felt. They had so much in common. Rocky was the sweet girl, the good girl, the quieter, shyer, more reserved girl – in fact, much like Zendaya. Rocky was a diligent student and nothing less than an A in her schoolwork would do. She dreamed of a future as a performer, of her dreams becoming a reality – much like Zendaya!

'I really felt Rocky,' Zendaya later revealed to *J-14* magazine. 'I have such a connection with her'.

Zendaya may have been living her dream but the filming schedule for *Shake It Up*, with early starts and late finishes, was relentlessly tough. On Wednesdays, the read-through for each episode took place, followed by rehearsals on Thursdays and Fridays, which included learning new dance moves. Weekends were spent perfecting these routines. The episodes were shot on Mondays and there would be live taping on Tuesdays. Then on Wednesdays, the same routine would begin all over again. However, Zendaya was in her element. There was no place she'd rather be. She loved working, loved being busy. She didn't 'do' spare time. That was lucky as there was precious little of it. In addition to the arduous *Shake It Up* schedule, Zendaya's schoolwork continued to be a priority. Like her character Rocky, perfectionist Zendaya wasn't happy unless she was achieving straight As in all her subjects. Officially, she was still attending Oak Hill High School but due to the long hours on *Shake It Up,* she and Bella took online classes and shared a tutor so that they were still able to receive an education while working. Every weekday meant five hours of schoolwork at the studio before the *Shake It Up* machine took over. By law, as long as the girls were achieving satisfactory grades, they could continue working. Nevertheless, conscientious Zendaya – even as a fourteen-year-old star-in-the-making – was not always happy with the standard of education she was receiving.

'I remember some kids I knew would cheat their way through an online school program,' she told *Glamour* magazine in 2017. 'They'd just look up the answers and type them in. That's insane to me. My mom got her master's in education. I think coming from a background in which education is so valued provided me with a sense of grounding. In this industry, there are always opportunities for someone to say that education is peripheral. There have been times when a lawyer has said, "All that's required is that you're provided with four walls and a human." And it was like, "Wait, but I actually *want* to excel in school."'

The situation was improved when Zendaya and her mother went head-to-head with Disney. They brokered a deal whereby a teacher was employed who met their exacting standards and who would also, as time went on, travel with Zendaya – and Bella – whenever they were required to travel to promote the show. After a hard day of both school and film work, there was little chance for Zendaya to relax in the evenings – not when she had homework and lines to learn.

'For me, homework always comes first, even before my "day job" on *Shake It Up*,' she wrote in *Between U and Me*. 'Education is top priority, so I will study and get my reports done for school before I hit my script and start memorizing Rocky's lines. I don't love homework but I'm not a homework hater, either. I tell myself that this is my chance to work independently and show how mature and responsible I can be. The smarter you are, the more you can handle. So, bring it on ...'

But no matter how mature and responsible she was aiming to be, how confident and self-assured, Zendaya was still just a thirteen-year-old girl and facing the kind of normal challenges all girls of that age face. Dealing with her monthly period, for instance. She was living with her father in an apartment in downtown Los Angeles and, although she loved him dearly, she wanted her mother. Zendaya had her first period while she was on-set and Kazembe was at a loss over what to do, even though he had older daughters. When shopping in the supermarket to buy his youngest what she needed, the vast range of sanitary protection on offer was mind-boggling and, feeling stressed out, he called Zendaya's teacher in the hope she would talk him through just what to purchase. He ended up cutting out the middleman – himself – and putting the store assistant on the line to Zendaya's teacher. Missing her mother, Zendaya would often video-call Claire while she was teaching so it would feel like she was with her. It was a weird transitional phase and there were occasions when Zendaya felt decidedly wobbly. Life would, she knew, be so much simpler if she returned to Oakland and lived the same kind of life as most girls of her age. She could hang out with her friends, go to normal high school, live with both parents in the family home, spend time with her siblings and their kids, her dog … and lead a regular kind of teenage life. There were times when, exhausted with her schedule, she craved this kind of normality. Certainly, neither parent insisted that she continue. Anything but. Both Kazembe and Claire would tell her that she could go back to Oakland whenever she wanted, and they could all take up their former lives. But, when it came to it, as hard as it was at times, Zendaya was determined to power on through. This was the kind of life she'd craved for years.

On 7 November 2010, *Shake It Up* debuted its first episode with a whopping 6.2 million views. It was, at the time, the second highest rated series premiere in Disney history. Zendaya had started to be recognized even before the show went out – and she loved it. While getting frozen yogurt at an LA shopping mall, she was approached by a little girl who had seen *Shake It Up* promoted on the Disney Channel. The girl asked for a photo, which Zendaya was only too delighted to pose for. She then returned the favour by asking her young fan for a pic as she was the first person ever to recognize her!

Once *Shake It Up* had aired, the tween and teen magazines became cheerleaders for the show, Rocky and CeCe – or rather Zendaya and Bella.

'*Shake It Up* is a one-stop shop for comedy, adventure and dance excitement!' enthused *Glitter* magazine. 'The theme song is performed by another Disney starlet, Selena Gomez, proving girl power can find its home at the Disney Channel! A certain fan favourite with crazy antics and relatable characters, *Shake It Up* is the perfect television show for girls of all ages. Bella & Zendaya are super in-tuned with their fans because they are girls just like you!'

The popularity of the show was the icing on the cake for Zendaya. It was everything she'd ever hoped for – and then some.

'Words cannot express how crazy this is, I mean, I am ecstatic!' she said when interviewed for *Glitter* magazine shortly after the series premiered. 'I am overjoyed, and I just hope it continues forever and ever and ever. Every day I am living my dream with *Shake It Up*.'

The show's young viewers couldn't get enough of Rocky, CeCe, their adventures, exploits and dance-athons. As the success of the show grew, so did Zendaya and Bella's celebrity – and at an extraordinary speed. Within weeks of the show premiering, the music video for the *Shake It Up* theme song was released. The next few months saw the girls appearing on radio shows, at charity events, red carpet events and movie premieres. It was at a Justin Bieber red carpet event in early 2011 – the premiere of his film *Never Say Never*, to be precise – that Zendaya, looking uber cool in an on-trend metallic jacket and patent mini skirt, was first styled by soon-to-be-legendary fashion stylist and image architect Law Roach. He would go on to curate and design some of her most iconic looks. On the red carpet, Zendaya – with her father hovering in the background in his combined role as father/manager/bodyguard

– was a bubbling confection of teenage excitement and cool professionalism.

'It will be overwhelming but I'm ready for it,' she said, referring to the runaway success of Shake It Up and how she envisaged it would impact on her life. 'So long as I have my family, I'll be good. My life is changing. I'm at this huge premiere and I'm starting to get recognized. That was so weird at first, but now little kids are starting to recognize me on the street and I love it – and girls my own age and it's really cool. I feel so loved.'

With Shake It Up rapidly becoming TV's number one series with kids, tweens and young teens, the next few months were a whirlwind for Zendaya and the rest of the cast. They appeared on Good Morning America to dance and talk about their show. They performed the Shake It Up theme tune with fellow Disney princess Selena Gomez at an industry event. In Spring 2011, another dream came true for Zendaya when she and Bella travelled to Paris, France, to promote the show. Meanwhile, Zendaya's talents as a singer were coming to the fore. In June, her and Bella's single 'Watch Me' was released, peaking at number 63 on the Billboard Hot Digital Songs chart and number 86 on the Billboard Hot 100. However, Zendaya had already, a month earlier, released the solo 'Swag It Out', a promotional independent single which, she said, was a song about self-esteem. The music video, shot in her native Oakland, was released on Zendaya's YouTube channel a few months later, showing the fifteen year old looking the height of cool in a pair Daisy Dukes and a hot pink and black cropped jacket decorated with a giant 'Z'. She also assisted the director of the video. So … just what was the 'swag' factor?

'Your own personal style, your personal aura,' she told ClevverTV. 'Everyone has their own swag.' 'Swag' was very much a Zendaya thing. She was, in fact, swag personified. And she was becoming known to her rapidly growing legion of fans – who dubbed themselves 'Zswaggers' – as the ultimate style icon.

'When I moved out to LA, I changed my style,' she wrote in *Between U and Me*. 'I got a lot more funky, a lot more fun and brought that to *Shake It Up*, plus they had so many cool ideas – amazing designers. Sometimes they put things together and you don't know how it'll work but when they come together it's like the best thing ever.'

Zendaya would take on board the *Shake It Up* designers' advice and bring it home with her. There she would experiment – mixing and matching colours, prints, stripes, polka dots, everything ... Her style secret was to wear clothes that suited her body and her personal style. It was vital you felt good about what you wore. She also loved dressing as Rocky – their style was similar – although Zendaya felt Rocky was a little more girly than she was. For example, Zendaya might, for her own look, take one of Rocky's cute, ruffly skirts and rock it up with tights, combat boots and a leather jacket. It was all about mixing – or swagging – it up and not opting for predictable pairings, shapes, textures and colours. Not when there were so many permutations and possibilities. Zendaya's fashion and style tips have stood the test of time and are as relevant today as they were back when she was a tween, proving that she's always been sartorially savvy. As a kind of fashion chameleon, she changed her look regularly, regarding it as a really good thing, trying out new styles and discovering what made her feel and look good. For Zendaya, fashion was – and still is – all about being inventive. Mixing colours, patterns and textures to create something new and exciting and very much her own. She likened it to starring in her own version of *Project Runway* every day, but her underlying fashion philosophy was simple: be who you are and don't be afraid to experiment. She was proving this time and time again on *Shake It Up*, but also on her increasingly stylish appearances on the red carpet.

The Disney Channel capitalized on Zendaya's 'swag factor' when, in summer 2011, it launched an affordable thirty-five-piece clothing line for the US store Target, based on Rocky and CeCe's signature looks. Unlike other television merchandizing spin-offs, the characters' likenesses were not portrayed on the items. Instead, the mix and match pieces were inspired by Rocky and CeCe's looks and personalities, comprising clothes you might find in their wardrobes and drawers. Uber-trendy pieces mixing patterns and fabrics that created a fun and fearless look. Ultra-cool, rebel blacks punched up with electric green, fuchsia and deep purples. Sequins, grommets and studs accenting animal prints and dark mottled tie-dye which, when combined, resulted in a perfect, dance-ready look.

'It's amazing – so awesome that kids get to dress up as their favourite characters on TV,' Zendaya proclaimed from the red carpet at a Disney event soon after the collection was launched. 'We're so excited that we can see little girls dressed up like Rocky and CeCe.'

A few months later, Disney launched a line of VIP *Shake It Up* dolls inspired by Rocky and CeCe and dressed in ultra-hip, urban-inspired fashions from the show. The VIP tag referred to the purchasers of the dolls rather than the stars or characters. Each 'Rocky' and 'CeCe' boxed figure came with a VIP card embossed with a special code, allowing the buyers to go online and get exclusive video content. As of 2023, Rocky and CeCe dolls are listed on eBay and similar sites for hundreds of dollars.

The runaway success of *Shake It Up* meant that a second season was pretty much a given. It had been announced in March 2011, filming started that July and the first episode of season two was aired two months later. Fans couldn't wait to see what best buddies CeCe and Rocky would get up to next. The fact that Zendaya and Bella seemed really close off the set made their on-screen partnership even more magical. But off-screen, things were not quite as they seemed. In fact, it emerged some years later that during the first season, the girls – contrary to the best-buddy closeness they exuded and spoke of in interviews – were not so friendly after all. Essentially, they were forced to compete with one another. To outdo each other. It didn't help that at the time their personalities, in contrast to the PR put out by the Disney Channel, also clashed.

In a 2020 interview with *J-14*, Bella Thorne related how they had actually got off to a 'rocky' start during the first season of *Shake It Up*. 'Zendaya and I were put in a very unfortunate position where we were kind of forced to compete against each other, which made the whole first season of the show just very awkward for us. We were constantly being put against each other. It was, "Who's better at this?" and "Who's better at that?". That fed into our heads. It made us not [be] friends in that first season.'

In the second season, however, matters improved. The girls had a kind of 'tell-all' talk where they both started crying and laid everything out on the table. After the heart-to-heart they genuinely did become best friends.

The second season of *Shake It Up* premiered in September 2011 and promised to explore the personalities and lives of Rocky and CeCe in greater depth. Zendaya was happy that the characters were being explored more deeply and that the issues they were faced with were more realistic.

'Real issues that teenage girls and families and people all over the world have to deal with,' Zendaya revealed in several publicity interviews for the show. 'It's really nice to see that Rocky and CeCe are not perfect, they have problems. They go through the same things that everyone else goes through and they have to deal with them. I like that it makes our characters real and more relatable to everyone out there.'

As was predicted when *Shake It Up* first broadcast, Zendaya and Bella were both becoming more and more recognized – something both girls clearly relished.

'I actually have a lot of fun fan encounters,' related Zendaya in an interview for AssignmentTX.com. 'There's been times when I've been at amusements parks and kids cry. It's amazing. I think every encounter with a fan is special. Every single fan is special. I always try my best to see as many as possible, even when I'm trying to rush or go somewhere, I try to stop and make sure I do that as that is why I am doing this. They are why I have my job.'

In an interview from *Glitter* magazine from around this time, Zendaya was asked where she saw herself in five years' time. 'There are so many things I want to do,' she replied. 'I really want to act in a feature film, put out an album, go on tour, design clothes, write a book, walk the runway … basically everything!'

In other words, conquer the world – and nothing, but nothing, was going to stop her!

A Match Made in Fashion Heaven

A certain alchemy was at work the day Law Roach first crossed paths with Zendaya Coleman. Without his unique talent as a fashion stylist and image architect, without his creative vision and all-round sartorial input into her career journey, it is debatable that she would have become the megastar she is today.

Their initial meeting took place in 2011, when Zendaya was just fourteen years old and filming the first series of *Shake It Up*. Law, who then owned a vintage store in his native Chicago, had arrived in Los Angeles to go on a personal shopping session for a customer. A customer who just happened to be a friend of a friend of Zendaya's and her dad, Kazembe.

'The day I arrived, a beautiful girl came by with her dad, and it was Zendaya,' Law recalled to the UK newspaper *The Guardian*.

This was the beginning of a match made in high fashion

heaven, one which would go on to see the two fulfil their fearsomely full potential as they grew together, building simultaneous careers.

Born Lawrence Roach in July 1978, life wasn't easy as the eldest of five children growing up on Chicago's South Side. In fact, it was decidedly tough, with a chaotically fractured family background – Law never really knew his father, while his mother didn't do rules where her kids were concerned. He would only attend school when he felt like it. At fourteen years old, he started staying with a friend, and he credits this oasis of stability and structure for helping him finish high school.

'My situation at home wasn't the best,' he told *Chicago* magazine in 2020. 'I grew up in a tough neighbourhood, in a school that was full of gangs. I don't know what saved me. I just always knew something bigger was coming.'

From an early age, Law was obsessed with the idea of women as icons, especially once he'd discovered Diana Ross's classic films of the 1970s: *Lady Sings the Blues*, *The Wiz* and *Mahogany*. He adored how retro and 1970s-chic Ross looked in these films. He also loved the fashion paraded on the reruns of vintage televisions series, such as *Dynasty* and *Charlie's Angels*. It was his grandmother Eloise who introduced him to the art of vintage shopping, or what she called 'junking', at local thrift stores. He would look through the women's racks out of curiosity but then started buying items that caught his eye. As his collection grew, he began lending pieces out to his most fashion-savvy girlfriends, and when they starting fighting over pieces at makeshift boot sales, where he had set up shop, Law realized a business opportunity was staring him in the face. He started selling his vintage finds, eventually opening a store in Chicago that he named Deliciously Vintage. A turning point came in 2009, when Kanye West visited the shop and bought several thousand dollars' worth of garments and accessories for his then-girlfriend, Amber Rose. As a result, suddenly stylists were flocking in from across the USA and from international capitals, such as Paris and London, asking Law to source all manner of vintage gems. It was Kanye's endorsement that emboldened Roach to establish himself as a fashion professional.

Until Zendaya met Law, she'd shopped predominantly at the bargain chain store Target for her clothes. But once he was in her life, all that changed. After their first encounter, Law took her shopping for an outfit for Justin Bieber's *Never Say Never* premiere. The resulting look was, in the words of Law himself: 'a puke green, patent leather Alexander Wang skirt with a silver Alice and Olivia blazer. We were like, "People are either gonna love it or hate it, but we love it,"' he told *The Guardian*. Ditto everyone else – most importantly, LA's style gurus and fashion influencers. After the appearance on the *Never Say Never* red carpet, Zendaya and Law became inseparable, joining forces in a promise to help each other and have each other's backs at a time when they were both struggling to receive recognition in their careers. They even joined pinkie fingers in a vow to be there for each other. But to begin with, it wasn't easy getting designers to dress Zendaya – she just wasn't well known enough, and Disney kids weren't taken seriously by either the film or fashion industries. However, Law had a plan to fix that: he started dressing her in clothes that other celebrities had already worn. This move saw Zendaya receiving exposure in the 'Who Wore It Better' columns in weekly magazines. Zendaya invariably came out on top, and before long people were starting to notice her. Roach told TheNationalNews.com that she was his fashion soulmate and he'd finally found the person he could share and bounce ideas off and create with. He said she was a sponge when it came to fashion. 'She wants to learn and she wants to know what your references are,' he explained.

From this embryonic relationship, Law went on to curate Zendaya's most iconic looks, helping to mould her into a fashion powerhouse and a highly anticipated celebrity on the red carpet at major events, including the prestigious Met Gala. He would go on to collaborate with her when she brought out her own collections of footwear and then clothes. Meanwhile, he would also go on to forge a career for himself as the fashion world's go-to stylist, to become the must-have image architect with a social media following of millions. Law nurtured, embraced and encouraged Zendaya's innately sassy attitude towards fashion. He rejoiced in it, calling her brave and giving her confidence to develop her own look and style. Without Law having by her side, she would never have felt courageous enough to sound off about her sartorial choices to the media and how she wasn't interested in following the fashion flock – especially in the earlier days of her career.

'I've gotten to a point in fashion where I just don't care,' she told PopSugar in 2016. 'I wear and do what I want because I like it, because I am confident in it, because it makes me feel good. That's the only way you can do it. The greatest of the greats are only great because they did what they wanted. And they didn't allow people's opinions to destroy who they are and stop them from being themselves.'

But in March 2023, Law shocked the fashion and entertainment world when he announced his retirement. 'My cup is empty,' he posted on Instagram. 'Thank you to everyone who've supported me and my career over the years. Every person that trusted me with their image, I'm so grateful for you all. If this business was just about the clothes, I would do it for the rest of my life but unfortunately, it's not! The politics, the lies and false narratives finally got me! You win ... I'm out.'

He went on to clarify his decision to *British Vogue*. 'I'm not saying I'm retiring from fashion,' he told the publication. 'I love fashion. I love the businesses, and I love being creative. What I'm retiring from is the celebrity styling part of it: the being in service and at service of other people. That's what I'm retiring from, yeah.'

He went on to explain in an interview with *E! News* that he had been unhappy for a while and felt the need to step away in order to concentrate on himself and what he wanted moving forward. Rumours were rife that Zendaya was responsible for this decision to step away: at the Louis Vuitton fashion show during Paris Fashion Week, Zendaya was seen sitting down on the front row next to fellow actor and LV ambassador Emma Stone, but there was no seat for Law. Zendaya gestured to the seat behind her – but rather than meaning that Law should sit there, she was in fact saying that this was her assistant Darnell's seat. Law clarified that he hadn't been angry with Zendaya, and he didn't feel that she was at all at fault – he had just been confused about where to sit. At no point did he blame his 'fashion soulmate' for the mix up. He took to Twitter to clear the air and explain where he and Zendaya stood in a series of tweets: 'So y'all really think I'm breaking up with Z..... we are forever!' Roach tweeted. 'She's my little sister and it's real love, not the fake industry love.'

Law, who has over a million Instagram followers, is in an enviable position as he considers what to do next and thinks about exploring new career options. He has strong relationships with designers like Valentino and is also championed by *British Vogue* editor-in-chief, Edward Enninful. Just twenty-four hours after posting about his retirement, he was strutting down the runway at a Boss fashion show in Milan with supermodel Naomi Campbell. Chatting backstage to *Vogue US* about this surprise move, he said, 'I am excited and nervous. And deeply grateful. I'm grateful that the Boss team sees me as more than just someone who dresses all these amazing celebrities.' Ouch!

Zendaya herself has not commented publicly on Law's retirement. But within days of his resignation, she was working with him again. How could she not?

'As a fourteen year old, I didn't know as much as I wanted to about the fashion industry – I just knew that I loved clothes and that I loved to express myself through clothes,' she recalled in an interview with Refinery29. 'Having him connecting that, teaching me about fashion and brands, I got the master course.'

Thankfully, she's still getting it!

THREE

Triple Threat

'Triple Threat: a person who is skilled in three different areas, especially a performer who can act, dance and sing well' – *Cambridge University Dictionary*

Due to the runaway success of *Shake It Up*, Zendaya was a bona fide Disney star, the darling of tweens and young teens everywhere. She was named in several polls as the best character from the series, but by 2012 she was beginning to emerge as much more. A triple threat in waiting, no less. It was only a matter of time before she would join the ranks of her heroine and fellow mononymous artist Beyoncé and the likes of Lady Gaga and Jennifer Lopez.

In January 2012, Zendaya's first feature film was released. Entitled *Frenemies*, the Disney movie also starred her *Shake It Up* 'sister', Bella Thorne. The film followed three pairs of teenage friends that go from friends to enemies and back again. Zendaya and Bella played one of the duos, Avalon Greene (Bella) and Halley Brandon (Zendaya), who create a web magazine called GeeklyChic. Their friendship is put to the test when they learn that a publishing company wants to take on their website but only wants one of them to stay on as senior editor. A review in *Channel Guide* magazine spoke of the film being, 'a universal message on the importance of friendship. It's relatable to everyone.' As with Rocky Blue, Zendaya found it easy to relate to Halley.

'Halley is a super smart girl and a great writer. She is really into fashion,' she told *Glitter* magazine. 'She is a good friend and slightly shy when it comes to talking in front of people. I can relate to her because I love to write just like Haley, and I am into many of the same things that she is.'

The reviews were, for Zendaya at least, promising: 'Zendaya succeeds at portraying Halley as a geeky character with a unique sense of style,' hailed the Screen Rant website. 'She is able to show confidence in anything she wears and any scene she is in.'

Zendaya had already broken out of her *Shake It Up* bubble by voicing the character of the garden fairy 'Fern' in Disney's *Pixie Hollow Games*, which premiered in late 2011. As with Rocky and Halley, Zendaya could relate to 'organized and practical' Fern, as she, too, possessed these qualities in abundance. She enjoyed the voice-over experience immensely. It was a totally different experience in which she used only her voice as opposed to the intense physicality of *Shake It Up*. She had to convey the message of the film and her character's personality purely by intonation and tone. It was a challenge, but one that Zendaya welcomed – just like she welcomed every challenge where her career was concerned. She had also guest starred in episodes of other Disney Channel shows, including *Good Luck Charlie*, in which she played her *Shake It Up* character, Rocky Blue, and *A.N.T. Farm*, where she portrayed a crazy teenage superstar named Sequoia Jones. Her singing career was blossoming, too. The second *Shake It Up* soundtrack, *Shake It Up: Live 2 Dance*, was released on 20 March 2012 with 'Something to Dance For', a solo track by Zendaya, released two weeks earlier.

Shake It Up season two concluded in August 2012 with a film-length final episode entitled 'Made in Japan' – but the cast and crew didn't actually travel to the land of the rising sun to film. Tokyo was recreated in the *Shake It Up* studio in Hollywood, where it was filmed in ten days in February 2012. The storyline focuses on CeCe and Rocky winning a dance competition, which leads them to travelling to Japan to make a video game. Rocky is keen to sightsee and experience Japanese culture but CeCe is all about the celebrity trappings and stardom factor. This causes the necessary drama between the pair. Zendaya was super excited about the special as she and Bella were able to sing almost as much as they danced, most memorably in a karaoke number. It really showed off Zendaya's vocal range – and her increasingly impressive sartorial style.

'There's a big song for the finale where I wear a classic, Betsey Johnson dress,' she told *Seventeen* magazine. 'It's edged up with a mini letterman jacket and some really cute Doc Martens that were actually custom-made for the movie. They have little black crystals on them and are so cute. I wish I got to keep them!'

On 21 August 2012, the extended edition of *Shake It Up: Made in Japan* was released with three new songs and a music video. 'Fashion Is My Kryptonite' had been released on 20 July 2012 as a promotional single with an accompanying music video, which was released on 3 August 2012. The soundtrack was the best-selling soundtrack of the year. Thanks to the success of *Shake It Up*, Zendaya landed herself a lucrative recording deal with Hollywood Records – previously the label of artists such as Selena Gomez and the Jonas Brothers. Working on her debut album became a priority and in this, as in every other area of her work – and, indeed, her life – she was her usual Virgoan perfectionist self. It had to be right and a combination of the kind of music she loved. Her vision was to create music that she was genuinely into, she explained while on the red carpet of the American Music Awards 2012, going on to say that there was no way she would be happy releasing material she wasn't a 100 per cent enthusiastic about. If she didn't love it and want to listen to it over and over, then why should her fans or anyone else? And it wouldn't be just dance-centric pop, either. She wanted her music to be different and speak to everyone. She was aiming to combine hip-hop, rock, pop and even country. For the awards ceremony, Zendaya had experimented with yet another new style. She looked retro-chic in a knee-length tulle skirt, fitted boat neck-style top and ankle-strap pumps. She also rocked a faux bob hairstyle which complimented the look to perfection.

Although Bella Thorne played the character billed as the leading role in *Shake It Up*, the truth was that Zendaya was emerging as the bigger star. Proof in this particular showbiz pudding came when she was featured in *Teen Vogue*'s Hollywood issue in September 2012 as one of their 'Stars on the Rise'. In the piece, a brief synopsis of her career to date was accompanied by some stunning circus-cum-wild-west themed images. Looking svelte and statuesque in all her 5 feet 10 inches (178 cm) of glory, she could easily have passed for a top model.

'The best birthday present ever!' she posted on Twitter and Instagram about her inclusion in the elite line-up. Now sweet sixteen, Zendaya was so excited to be included, she was on the point of buying up every issue of the magazine she could lay her hands on until her mother managed to stop her. Sporting Chanel-inspired art on her fingernails, she positively shimmered on the red carpet at *Teen Vogue*'s Young Hollywood Party, again proving her fashion prowess by wearing an on-trend vintage gold pleated maxi skirt and crisp white shirt. Zendaya stole the red-carpet show. She also impressed with her aura of cool sophistication, coming across as far more mature than her sixteen years. This was a very different Zendaya to the giggling, over-excited, over-exuberant and keen-to-please girl of just eighteen months earlier. This, one sensed, was the real Zendaya – or at least her beginnings. She would later say that, when starting out on her Disney career, she had put on an act and tried to be who she thought she should be rather than who she really was.

'I felt I had to make a persona that matched Rocky,' she said in 2017, while watching old videos of herself on YouTube, her head in her hands in embarrassment. 'All that, "Hey this is Zendaya – this is a place for happy, smiley faces … !" I had an entire alter ego and was so obnoxious. It was so fake.'

Maybe so in retrospect, but it hadn't seemed like that the time. The older Zendaya was perhaps being a tad too hard on her younger self. What girl in her early teens – dazzled by the kudos that came with being a Disney child star and uber-excited about what was happening in her young life – wouldn't have reacted in such a way? But at sixteen and a *Teen Vogue* 'One to Watch', perhaps, deep down, the novelty of being a Disney kid was beginning to lose a little of its original lustre-like sheen. She was maturing and wishing – in true Zendaya fashion – to take on new challenges and make the very best of her considerable talents. She was emerging as a glittering star, yet she refreshingly continued to prove that she was still very much the product of her two grounded parents.

'I think the biggest compliment I've received in my career is that people tell me I'm down to earth and humble,' she told *Glitter* magazine. 'I feel really good about that … I don't want to be considered anything other than that!'

The filming of season three of *Shake It Up* was still ongoing, with shooting not ending until March 2013. Despite her burgeoning career as a singer and emergence as a style icon, when interviewed, Zendaya remained as enthusiastic about the show and Rocky Blue as ever.

'She is a wonderful character and I just love her,' she told *Glitter* magazine. '*Shake It Up* is such a blessing to me and I am so lucky to work with great people and such a talented cast.'

Certainly, Zendaya's fans, her 'Zswaggers', had taken both her and her uber-sympathetic character to their hearts. So much so that her book *Between U and Me: How to Rock your Tween Years with Style and Confidence* was published in 2013. It was a kind of guide in which Zendaya shared her wit and wisdom on everything from fashion to friendships, family matters and following dreams, and, of course, affairs of the heart.

'I wanted to write something that would actually be useful,' she told MTV while publicizing the book, which had been inspired by the actual questions Zendaya had received from her millions of Facebook, Instagram and Twitter followers. 'It's something you can pick up and put right down.'

She wanted to reach out to the tween demographic who watched her and looked up to her as a role model. The tween years and early teens are awkward – you're no longer a little kid yet you're not a proper teenager either. Talking to parents was good but sometimes they didn't seem to recall that they, too, had once been twelve or thirteen.

'I wanted to maybe help with little things kids go through,' Zendaya revealed in numerous online and print interviews for the book. 'Things at school and also more serious things. It's a kinda guidebook written in my own words, it's very natural and it feels like I'm talking to the reader. It's not awkward but very personal. It's about my own experiences. I feel like I had good tween years. You know, I'm a normal kid and I still went to school at that time, still had regular stuff going on. I'm trying to be like the big sister.'

Although Disney did not officially announce until July 2013 that there wouldn't be a season four of *Shake It Up*, rumours had been rife since March that the show would be cancelled. No start date had been announced for filming, plus the channel did have a history of axing popular shows after a few seasons. *Good Luck Charlie* is just one example. Other young performers might have used the time to rest on their considerable laurels, hang out by the pool or beach and just party! Not Zendaya. She decided instead to utilize the months she would normally have been filming for the next season of *Shake It Up* to throw herself into something totally new. In addition to being busy recording her debut album, she signed up for the sixteenth series of ABC's *Dancing with the Stars*. At sixteen, she was, at the time, the youngest contestant ever to participate on the high-ratings entertainment show.

'I just want to try new things and put myself out there,' she told *Access Hollywood*. Zendaya was a dancer – but a hip-hop dancer. Ballroom dancing was a different kind of discipline altogether. It was the exact opposite of what she was used to. Not only would she have to learn the genre from scratch, but she'd also need to unlearn what she already knew. She was paired with Ukrainian-born world champion dancer Valentin 'Val'

Chmerkovskiy, who had joined the show two years earlier. She was thrilled at being coupled up with Val. He'd had an awesome previous season of *DWTS* and finished third. She had herself one good dancing partner. One of the best.

Val was equally delighted at having Zendaya as his celebrity partner: 'I was very excited,' he said in a *Dancing with the Stars* interview. 'We start from "Hi – I'm Val" and we go from there. You know, baby steps. I know she has a background in performing but it's a very different genre to what we have going on here and I'm educating her on certain angles and delivery points and just letting things grow organically.'

When Val asked Zendaya if she felt intimidated by being the youngest on the show, she admitted that she did a little bit because it felt like being the youngest girl in the playground at school. Val reassured her that it didn't matter if she was sixteen or thirty-six – she had nothing to be afraid of. In typical Zendaya style, she absorbed the training he gave her and took it home, where she practised and rehearsed over and over again. She was determined to prove that although she was the youngest, she could be as good as any of the other contestants. It was scary but she would just throw herself into it, work as hard as she could and do her very best. Val certainly gave her the reassurance she needed. He was super impressed by her dedication and work ethic, telling her she was awesome and that he thought they had bags of potential. He was right about that. Zendaya smashed it from the start. She and Val topped the leader board for the first three weeks of the competition with Val calling her 'an amazing, incredible student who was really talented with great energy and focus.'

The judges were equally impressed, with Carrie Anne Inaba commenting that Zendaya was a fantastic dancer with a maturity that was unexpected in a sixteen year old. 'A star is born. Big time!' Bruno Tonioli exclaimed after a difficult jive routine in week two of the competition, which earned Zendaya the first 'nines' of the season. She worked hard to learn new dances like the samba, the quickstep, the foxtrot and the salsa. Learning and perfecting a new dance style and complex choreography, performing live each week and awaiting the public vote was stressful. Plus, Val could be a hard task master at times. He later admitted that he'd been authoritative and strict with Zendaya, at one point challenging her every move and clapping his hands for emphasis while he was talking, which caused the room to fall silent. However, having him as a partner was key to her success. Val had a reputation for being a tough coach, for ruthlessly critiquing form and expecting the best. While this approach wouldn't have worked for every contestant on the show, it was effective for Zendaya due to her incredible work ethic and perfectionist personality. Val didn't just want her to be good, he wanted her to be incredible. Every week. And he knew very well that she had it in her.

'Zendaya was a special talent, and special talents have a special, higher bar to clear,' he later wrote in his 2018 memoir, *I'll Never Change My Name*. 'The standard was set not by the outside world, but by Zendaya herself, because of her talent. But it wasn't talent that would allow her to succeed, rather it was her desire to fulfil that talent to the best of her ability.'

Zendaya fully accepted Val's challenging coaching techniques, relentless rehearsal regime and desire to see her do well. However, the professional dancer's tough-love teaching style didn't always go down well her father, Kazembe.

'"I wanted to kill you, man," Kazembe told me later,' Chmerkovskiy wrote in *I'll Never Change My Name*. '"I'd never heard anybody speak to my daughter that way. Only I speak to my daughter that way. But I couldn't criticize or say anything to you because you know what? That's exactly what I would have told her. You were saying the kind of things that I tell her."'

Zendaya was changing. She was taking more charge of her destiny rather than relying on the advice of others. Kazembe would later say that Zendaya's involvement in *Dancing with the Stars* was the first time in her career that she told him she didn't want to do anything else while performing on the show. She wanted to give it absolutely everything she'd got. In all honestly, it was highly doubtful she would have had much to give to other projects anyway. She was still having to study, and there were occasions when she fell asleep while doing schoolwork because she was so tired from learning new complicated dance routines, rehearsing and performing. There was no 'off' time for her, but Zendaya powered her way through. Though the pressures of the competition increased week by week, Zendaya held her ground while remaining very much her own person. Mindful of the fact that her legions of tween fans would be watching her compete, she laid down a few ground rules from the off. She refused to have spray tans and insisted on having a say in the costumes she wore.

'They show a lot of skin on that show,' Zendaya explained to HuffPost Live. 'I wanted to make sure that all my outfits were appropriate because there's young girls watching me, and I want to make sure they can see that you can be beautiful without having to show everything.'

As the contest went on, Zendaya and Val frequently vied for the number one spot with country singer Kellie Pickler and her professional partner Derek Hough, sometimes topping the leader board, sometimes coming second. Three pairings competed against each other in the *DWTS* final on 21 May 2013: Zendaya and Val, Kellie and Derek, and NFL wide receiver Jacoby Jones and his professional partner Karina Smirnoff.

Zendaya's mother Claire couldn't hide her pride in her daughter's achievement. 'When she's out on that dance floor, she's really living,' Claire said in an interview with *DWTS*. 'Her emotion just oozes out of her in such a natural way. And I'm so proud every time I watch her.'

Over the course of their partnership, Zendaya and Val had developed a deep, deep bond. 'This guy right here is way more than just a partner,' Zendaya said in an interview on the eve of the final. 'He's an inspiration, a role model, a teacher, but most importantly he's family. I got the best big brother. He's always got my back and never lets me fall … literally.'

However, an incident during rehearsals for the first leg of the final almost put the Zendaya/Val dream team in jeopardy. Shortly before the show went on air, Zendaya accidently elbowed Val just above his right eye causing a bleeding gash. He needed a total of fourteen stitches.

'It happens,' Val explained. 'I've been hit in the face many times before. I was nervous that I wouldn't be able to dance for legal issues. But I'm good, you know. I'm good and I want her to enjoy the moment and focus on herself.'

Zendaya was full of apologies but able to see the funny side, joking: 'There's no way he's going to forget me now – every time he looks in the mirror and sees that scar, he's going to remember me.'

In the second leg of the final, Jones and Smirnoff were voted off first, leaving Zendaya and Val and Pickler and Hough vying for the top spot. Both couples performed a jive, but it was Pickler and Hough who ended up champions and lifting the mirror ball. Although naturally disappointed, Zendaya yet again displayed a wisdom beyond her years, being as graceful as she was in defeat.

'You know it's just the beginning,' she said in her final *DWTS* interview after taking the silver medal position. 'You never look at it as the end or something that's negative. It's just a platform for me to continue my music and everything else that I have set up. So, I think it's a great start.'

She also paid tribute to her fans: 'Throughout this process my fans have been beside me the entire way,' she told *Access Hollywood*. 'Whenever I would feel down or stressed out about the competition, I would just scroll through my Twitter mentions and read the wonderful things that my fans would say.'

She later revealed that she wanted her young fans to know that it wasn't always about winning. That the experience of *DWTS* had taught her so much – life lessons that she would carry with her into the future.

It was Val who seemed more disappointed with the result. 'She worked so hard, and I really wanted her to lift that trophy and jump-start her career. And she didn't lift the trophy and I felt heartbroken about that,' he wrote in *I'll Never Change My Name*. 'I wish I could go back and have another chance at that season. But it jump-started her career anyway. That's when you learn that it's not necessarily always about winning or losing, it's really about learning through the process and then using those tools to further yourself down the road.'

For Zendaya, that road became rockier when, in July 2013, Disney officially announced the cancellation of *Shake It Up*. She had known, of course, that the end was on the horizon, but being Zendaya, she preferred to focus on the positives.

'Nothing lasts forever,' she told HuffPost Live, 'which is why you have to continue to invent yourself and do new things.'

Zendaya knew that whatever happened in the future she had a great support system in the form of her family. She also knew that the transition from being a Disney kid to an adult star could be tough.

'I think everyone's transition is different,' she further explained to HuffPost Live. 'I'm not really transitioning; I'm just growing up. It's all about having that support and good people around you and I definitely have that. I'm a good kid. I don't really have to worry about getting in trouble or whatever. I'm just a good kid and I'm just trying to spread that goodness to the younger generations.'

Zendaya's inner circle remained as tight as ever. She continued to dazzle on red carpets and regularly made the 'best dressed' lists, but she was never one for parties and, at heart, she remained true to her wholesome, family-orientated self, never allowing herself to be distracted or steered off course. Besides which, being highly perceptive, she could usually sniff out people on the make at twenty paces. And that's what her parents were there for, too. Naturally, they had her back and provided her with a very stable, extremely tight support system.

She had much to thank *Shake It Up* for – in fact, pretty much everything. However, as well as the success that had occurred in her professional life, there were rumours of romance. Although she had refused a lip-to-lip on-screen kiss on *Shake It Up* because she said she had yet to be kissed in real life, there has been speculation that the show saw her coupling up with a number of male co-stars during the three or so years she played Rocky. She wasn't officially allowed to date until her sixteenth birthday, which is something she would later say had been a good thing. But according to Heightline website, Adam Irigoyen, who played Deuce Martinez in *Shake It Up,* was her first boyfriend. College Candy claimed their relationship – if you can call it that when Zendaya was only thirteen and Adam a year younger – lasted for two years, but that was probably just the wishful thinking of her Zswaggers, who wanted to believe that two of their favourite TV stars were an item in real life. Heightline also linked Zendaya with Leo Howard, who played Logan Hunter in the show. Leo's character Logan dated Zendaya's Rocky in the show and again this is perhaps why Zendaya and Leo were mooted as a real-life couple. If they ever were, the 'relationship' is thought to have lasted only a few months at most. It was Heightline, yet again, that speculated over the identity of Zendaya's next squeeze. He wasn't a *Shake It Up* co-star but actor, rapper, singer, songwriter and dancer Trevor Jackson, who was something of a multiple threat himself. According to the website, Zendaya met him two years before they started dating in 2013, with their relationship lasting until 2017. This particular speculation, though, turned out to be true.

Fiercely private about her personal life (the only time she had ever alluded to it was when she had joked that any potential love interest would have to be run past her father and brothers before any kind of relationship could develop), Zendaya was keen to concentrate on her career. The lead single 'Replay' of her self-titled debut studio album *Zendaya* was released on 16 July 2013. The song peaked at forty on the Billboard Hot 100 and was certified platinum by the Recording Industry Association of America (RIAA). The album was released on 17 September 2013 and debuted on the Billboard 200 at number 51, selling around 7,458 copies in its first week.

'I'm kind of creating my own music and I'm kind of creating my own zone, my own lane as an artist,' she told MTV. 'I want to do rhythmic pop, it's not necessarily your average pop song. It has some kind of urban edge, some kind of more hip-hop-ish tones to it that kind of edge it up and do something a little different so it's not just your stereotypical pop music.'

To further promote the album, Zendaya performed on a variety of television shows and set out on a North American tour from June to December 2013.

Around this time, the question of college became something

of an issue within the Stoermer/Coleman household. Zendaya was due to graduate from Oak Hill High School in 2015, despite having completed nearly all of her schooling on-set. Ever the educator, Claire was keen for her daughter to attend college, but Kazembe had reservations. He argued that youngsters went to college to obtain the qualifications to secure a good job, but Zendaya already had a fantastic career and potentially even more fantastic prospects. Why interrupt the flow to attend college for three or four years and gain a degree? Experience told him that if Zendaya stepped off the showbusiness merry-go-round for that length of time, when she was ready to jump back on it, it might be too late. Her moment would have passed. He also argued that in her line of work, Zendaya was surrounded by experts in her field: successful and talented businesspeople, agents, filmmakers, TV executives and creatives. Who better to learn from than these at-the-top-of-their-game professionals? Plus ... Zendaya just happened to have some very promising offers on the table. Unlike her *Shake It Up* co-star Bella Thorne, she had decided not to sever ties with Disney. In August 2013, Zendaya had been cast as sixteen-year-old Zoey Stevens, the lead character in the Disney Channel original film *Zapped*. Then in November 2013, she was cast as the lead in a Disney Channel pilot called *Super Awesome Katy*. However, the title didn't stay that way for long. The reason? Zendaya didn't like it – nor was she happy with several other details about the production. And she was beginning to wield such power within the industry that whatever she said, went.

Eat (and Drink) to the Beat

When it comes to food and drink, Zendaya is a teetotal veggie, albeit one with a very sweet tooth. She first considered becoming vegetarian at the relatively early age of eleven. She had passed a slaughterhouse while on a road trip with her father and was horrified that animals inside were waiting to be killed so that humans could eat them. It was a light bulb moment: it was the first time she properly realized where the meat on her dinner plate and in her burger came from. However, while she was now more aware of how animals were treated for human consumption, she did not officially become a vegetarian until she watched PETA's 2009 graphic documentary *Glass Walls*, a production narrated by Sir Paul McCartney and known for his quote: 'If slaughterhouses had glass walls, everyone would be vegetarian.' For the first few days – or rather nights – after deciding to turn veggie, she would have crazily vivid dreams about hamburgers and giant meat dishes raining down on her from the sky, likening it to the book and film *Cloudy with a Chance of Meatballs.*

It wasn't long, however, before her sleep became a sausage-and-steak-free zone as she stopped craving meat and fish. She didn't like the taste – or even imagining the taste. She said it made her feel weird, although she would occasionally still yearn for a taste of her mother's famous turkey burgers. At seventeen, Zendaya picked up another award when she was voted PETA's sexiest female vegetarian.

However, being vegetarian wasn't always a walk through the veg patch for her. The reason? She wasn't especially fond of vegetables and salad stuff. It's said that she still isn't to this day, plus she doesn't like to cook (apart from a pasta dish with avocado, which she invented one day when a solo 'butter pear' was the only thing she had in her fridge). Zendaya usually orders in when she's home in the evening.

'I just (a) don't like following directions, and I'm (b) too lazy,' she told *Harper's Bazaar*. 'It's a time thing, too. I order food in. I can have anything I want; that's the beauty of ordering food. If I'm having my favourite meal, I'll just skip right to ice cream. In fact, I get in trouble with my assistant a lot. He says I shouldn't do that.'

Oh my, does this girl just love ice cream! Especially coffee flavour. 'Don't even try to come between me and my Haagen Dazs,' she has tweeted on occasion. Maybe her penchant for ice cream is not surprising, considering her hidden talent of being able to bite into it with her two front teeth and not feel any nerve pain. She's said that anyone who spends time with her will start eating 'The Zendaya Diet' – that is, ice cream – on a daily basis. Sometimes even for breakfast. Not that she's a big brekkie fan. When she does have it, usually at her assistant Darnell's bidding, it will be something like pancakes, berries and, being a self-confessed chocoholic, Nutella. But she has never liked syrup on her pancakes, much preferring butter.

Until recently, her favourite lunch dish was instant noodles with hot sauce, but she stopped eating them when she realized the noodle seasoning contained chicken powder and therefore some semblance of poultry. These days, her favourite quick and easy, go-to DIY lunch is a veggie rice salad, where she combines instant brown rice, vegetable broth, olive oil and sautéed veggies – onion, courgette (or zucchini to Zendaya), mushrooms and carrots – with lemon juice, salt and pepper. That is, when she remembers to have lunch: 'It's bad but because I work so much, sometimes I forget to eat. I snack throughout the day, though, especially if I'm on-set,' she revealed to *Harper's Bazaar*. She also enjoys her mother's vegetarian lasagne, but then who doesn't love their own mother's home-cooking?

You can take the girl out of Oakland, but you can't take the Oakland out of the girl, and this girl just loves her fast food. On her website, Zendaya.com, she posted her vegetarian guide to fast food in 2020, which reads like an ode to where to grab-and-go delicious vegetarian dishes from the most popular fast food chains in the USA.

'Think a vegetarian can't go to basically any fast-food joint and order up a storm? Think again!' read the post. 'Most days I order fast food and I've found a way to satisfy my veggie diet just about anywhere.'

At In-N-Out Burger, she recommended getting the grilled cheese with grilled onions and extra spread and the animal-style fries, commenting that, 'The grilled onions are the perfect add-on and while the animal-style fries are messy as hell, they are so delish.' At Chick-Fil-A, Zendaya's go-to takeaway was listed as a Spicy Southwest Salad, minus the chicken; at Panda Express she bigged-up the veggie spring rolls and stir-fry mixed veg; a Veggie Delite sandwich was her choice at Subway; while her favourite Chipotle dish was the 'make your own salad bowl of cilantro-lime white rice, black beans, romaine lettuce, guacamole, cheese and tomato salsa – can't say enough about the mix of flavors in this one. Ridiculously good!'

To help her achieve her daily vitamin and mineral requirements, Zendaya is said to take a daily multivitamin, plus an omega-3 supplement for its cardiovascular benefits.

As for drinks, Zendaya has never drunk alcohol – not even on her twenty-first birthday in September 2017, when she could legally drink in the USA for the first time. She was never interested and has said she doesn't plan to start drinking. She has felt her life is stressful enough as it is and doesn't see how relaxing with a cocktail would help. Keeping her wits about her at all times is important to her, so she is in no danger of losing control or making the wrong decisions. She also hasn't wanted drinking to become a vice. Her opinion has been 'Why try something if you don't need it?' But you also won't find her sipping on green juices or hot water with lemon. She liked – and still likes – regular juices and lemonade, preferably home-made. Water, of course. But never energy drinks, soda or coffee. And she just adores an iced matcha green tea latte with coconut milk. Who doesn't?

FOUR

A Shero

'To me, locs are a symbol of strength and beauty, almost like a lion's mane' –
Zendaya after the Oscars, February 2015

In a 2017 interview with *Vogue* magazine, Kazembe Coleman gave a unique insight into the steely determination already hard-wired into his daughter when she was still just a toddler. He was recalling Thanksgiving 1998 and how little two-year-old Zendaya had been acting up at her grandmother's dining table. When she didn't let up, give in or start playing nice, Kazembe suddenly announced they were going straight home. 'Got a block away from home before she finally gave up,' he recalled. 'Man, she was two. She's a tough one, man.'

Nowhere was this innate toughness better illustrated than in how Zendaya dealt with the Disney Channel when she had been offered the title role in their new series *Super Awesome*

Katy. Disney proposed that Katy would be a high school student following in the footsteps of her seemingly normal parents, who just happened to be secret spies on the side. Zendaya was interested. She wasn't quite ready to leave the protective stable that the Disney Channel had provided, plus the basic premise of the show was promising. However, Zendaya made it clear from the get-go that she would only consider taking on the role if certain, quite specific, conditions were met with regards to the nature and personality of her character – she didn't want her to be another Rocky Blue. She had suspicions that after a few episodes the producers and writers would make this girl suddenly discover she could sing or dance, so Zendaya ensured that the character wouldn't be good at singing, dancing or in any way artistically inclined. There were other skills a fictional teenage girl on television could have and, indeed, would want to have. This kid should be smart – a bit of a brainiac, slightly nerdy, uncool and socially awkward, maybe a martial arts expert who could think on her feet. Anything a boy could do, this girl could do, too. She should be a regular kid but with an extraordinary secret life.

Zendaya wrote down all her ideas, wanting to create the vision she saw in her head. She demanded a name change for Katy, saying that a girl with a mixed-race heritage wouldn't realistically be given that name. 'Do I look like a Katy to you?' she reportedly asked Disney executives. 'We're changing that!' But Zendaya hadn't finished – in fact, she'd barely started! She insisted that the series primarily feature a family of colour. She knew how important it had been for her, as a kid growing up, to watch a show like *That's So Raven* on television. As a young person of a mixed ethnicity, it had been hard for her to see hardly anyone who looked like her or who came from a similar background on television – and she knew how difficult it *still* was for kids like her. Zendaya felt it was vital to see diversity on the Disney Channel. Simply put: either Disney agreed to what she wanted, or she wouldn't take the part. She felt it was high time the channel started to reflect what life was really like on the streets, towns and cities of America.

'I didn't feel like there was any other choice,' Zendaya explained in a later interview with *Glamour*. 'I was like, "If I'm going to do this, this is how it has to be." There *needs* to be a Black family on the Disney Channel. A lot of people who aren't people of color can't quite understand what it's like to grow up and not see yourself in mainstream media. And you know, there is so much work left to be done. I've talked about this before, but can I honestly say I would be in the position I'm in if I weren't a lighter-skinned Black woman? No.'

Last but not least, Zendaya insisted on being a producer on the show – ensuring that she had real control and input into the content. She was not yet seventeen years old. This was astonishing – and super awesome! The prospect of making such serious demands of such a huge corporation would have daunted stars many years her senior. But Zendaya, as she had proved time and time again, was a real force to be reckoned with. Negotiating so skilfully with people seemingly more powerful and much older than her didn't seem to faze her one bit. How was she not cowed by these mainly white, middle-aged men in suits? There was, as always, the innate confidence she had inherited from her parents, Claire and Kazembe, who had raised her to be a strong, caring, compassionate young woman and who had instilled in her the instinct to always be herself, because herself was more than good enough. However, this self-confidence is not something that she had acquired overnight.

'My number one thing is that it just doesn't happen,' she was to tell Complex website in 2015. 'You shouldn't feel discouraged if you're not waking up and feeling amazing about yourself. That's not necessarily how it works. It's a developing process. Everyone goes at their own speed … As long as you take every opportunity to learn more about yourself and fall more in love with yourself every day, you're doing good.'

For Zendaya there was nothing narcissistic about practising self-love. Rather it was non-negotiable.

'I would say my number one tip is to know that it's okay to be in love with yourself,' she revealed to PopSugar in 2016. 'That's not a bad thing. People might think it's cocky or arrogant or selfish – no, that's not what that means. Being in love with yourself is okay. You're allowed to love yourself first. That's who you're supposed to love.'

A savvy business woman already, Zendaya was also fully aware of her worth and star quality. She'd been a Disney star for almost four years. She knew the power she had at her immaculately manicured fingertips. What gave her an extra edge was that she was speaking on behalf of her millions of fans and followers. But far from it being a calculated, purely self-motivated career move, she was doing it for the increasingly diverse society she knew should be represented on mainstream television.

'A lot of people don't realize their power,' she later explained to *Cosmopolitan* magazine. 'I have so many friends who say yes to everything or feel like they can't stand up for themselves in a situation. No: you have the power.'

The execs agreed to all of Zendaya's terms. The show was renamed and now went by *K.C. Undercover* – Zendaya's character had become Katrina-Charlotte Cooper, hence the initials K.C. She had input in the content, including a future storyline about the controversial stop-and-frisk policing policy, making sure it was accessible for kids. Filming the pilot began in early 2014, with the first series confirmed that May. A month later, *Zapped*, the feature-length film Zendaya had made for Disney the previous year, was released. In this movie Zendaya's character, Zoey, struggles to adjust to her new school and life with her new stepfather and stepbrothers. But everything changes when a dog-training app on her phone begins controlling the men and boys around her. In short, Disney magic turns Zoey's mobile phone into a boy whisperer, allowing her to control their actions and behaviour. Zendaya bigged the movie up in the media, but the reviews were middling.

'Zendaya plays a high school student with the seriousness of a grad student. Even when she's manipulating others to her will, she doesn't seem to be even a little thrilled,' wrote *The New York Times*. 'Naturally, once everyone is behaving to Zoey's liking, their lives begin to collapse, which wreaks havoc on Zoey. Mainly [the film] is a vehicle for Zendaya, one tiny step in her impending ubiquity. She's been tapped to play Aaliyah in a Lifetime biopic, and she was recently named the face of Material Girl, the clothing line run by Madonna and her daughter, Lourdes.'

Zendaya had, indeed, been signed up as the face of Material Girl in June 2014. She spoke of Madonna's confidence and risk taking, and how she was able to set trends and do things other people couldn't. It was something Zendaya was trying (successfully) to emulate. She loved the clothes she was modelling, and getting to meet the original material girl, Madonna, was of course a high point. She and Lourdes were the same age, with only a month between them, so Zendaya was the perfect fit for the youth-focused line. 'I think it's really fun and very fashion-forward,' Zendaya said of the pieces. 'Not only that, but there are also a lot of cool quality pieces that are really affordable.'

However, the Aaliyah Lifetime biopic never materialized. Regarded as one of the most influential singers in the history of R&B, Aaliyah had quickly risen to prominence in the early 1990s. Dubbed the Princess of R&B, she sold an estimated 32 million albums worldwide and picked up several prestigious awards. But her life was cut tragically short when she was killed in a plane crash, aged just twenty-two, in August 2001. Given her lasting legacy in the music industry, it would only be a matter of time before her life was portrayed on film. The script for the biopic was based on the book *Aaliyah: More Than a Woman*, by Christopher Farley. Zendaya was set to record four of the songs in the film as well as to portray the life and legacy of the 'Back and Forth' singer. Zendaya initially agreed to play the late star, but she pulled out before production began. According to multiple reports, after the announcement of Zendaya playing the leading role, the family of Aaliyah pushed back against the project and Zendaya dropped out. There were rumours that Aaliyah's family considered Zendaya to be too light in colour to take on the role, and also that Aaliyah's fans were in uproar over the casting, considering Zendaya not talented enough to play their heroine. Finally, Zendaya addressed the reasons she had decided to back out of the biopic. On Instagram, she stated her case: 'Let me just explain something. The reason why I chose not to do the Aaliyah movie had nothing to do with the haters or people telling me I couldn't do it, that I wasn't talented enough or I wasn't black enough. It had absolutely nothing to do with that. The main reasons were that the production value wasn't there.'

There were also complications with the music rights, and Zendaya didn't think it had been handled delicately enough, considering the circumstances. She tried reaching out to the family and wrote a letter but heard nothing back. She then felt it just wasn't possible for her to move forward with the project and so she backed out. No matter. Another Material Girl campaign was on the cards, plus *K.C. Undercover* premiered in January 2015. Just as Zendaya had stipulated in her initial meetings with the Disney Channel, high school student Katrina-Charlotte 'K.C.' Cooper was a maths whiz with a black belt in karate. A normal teen otherwise, her life changed when her parents, accountants Craig and Kira, recruited her to be a spy, like them, in a secret government agency known as 'The Organization'. Along with her parents and younger siblings Ernie and Judy (the latter being a humanoid robot), K.C. had to balance a civilian existence with undercover missions designed to save the world. As K.C. embarked on her secret spy journey, it was vital she kept the secret from her best friend Marisa. Zendaya was happy with how both her character and the show had been developed. K.C. was a little geeky, a little awkward and not the most popular girl in school – in fact, a regular teenager – but she got to experience highly irregular and exciting things. Zendaya spoke glowingly of *K.C. Undercover* in publicity interviews, saying what a fun show it was and that it was great viewing for all the family – but with a lot of heart at its core. She was, she said, very proud of it. Again, she found parallels to the character she was playing in herself. Like K.C., Zendaya had two very different lives, her work life and her private life, which she was continually trying to balance.

Zendaya's instincts were spot on. However, rather than the new Disney series, it would be her appearance at the Oscars in February 2015 that would make massive headlines – and for highly controversial reasons. Zendaya attended the Academy Awards wearing a white silk off-the-shoulder Vivienne Westwood column gown, which she paired with waist-skimming locs (aka dreadlocks) pulled back into a half-up style. She looked stunning, with *Vogue* heralding her as the 'breakout style star' of the night and hailing her as 'one part Lisa Bonet, one part Venus de Milo, and all very grown up.' However, this was completely overshadowed by *E! News* anchor and *Fashion Police* host Giuliana Rancic, who made highly controversial comments about Zendaya's hair style. The locs, she said, made Zendaya look like someone who 'smells like patchouli oil and weed'.

Zendaya, eighteen and a half years old at the time, allowed the comments to sink in before responding. She instinctively knew that a knee-jerk reaction would be a wrong move. Once home, she sat in her room and fought the urge to send an angry tweet right away. She mulled things over before composing a reply. A self-confessed poor speller, she gave it to her mother, Claire, to proofread before posting on Twitter and Instagram. It was long and measured, mature and to-the-point.

'There is a fine line between what is funny and disrespectful,' it read. 'Someone said something about my hair at the Oscars that left me in awe. Not because I was relishing in rave outfit reviews, but because I was hit with ignorant slurs and pure disrespect. To say that an 18-year-old young woman with locs must smell of patchouli oil or "weed" is not only a large stereotype but outrageously offensive. I don't usually feel the need to respond to negative things but certain remarks cannot go unchecked. I'll have you know my father, brother, best childhood friend and little cousins all have locs. Do you want to know what Ava DuVernay (director of the Oscar nominated film *Selma*), Ledisi (nine times Grammy nominated singer/songwriter and actress), Terry McMillan (author), Vincent Brown (Professor of African and African American Studies at Harvard University), Heather Andrea Williams (Historian who possesses a JD from

Harvard University and an MA and PhD from Yale University) as well as many other men, women and children of all races have in common? Locs. None of which smell of marijuana. There is already harsh criticism of African Americans in society without the help of ignorant people who choose to judge others based on the curl of their hair. My wearing my hair in locs on an Oscar red carpet was to showcase them in a positive light, to remind people of color that our hair is good enough. To me, locs are a symbol of strength and beauty, almost like a lion's mane. I suggest some people should listen to India Arie's 'I Am Not My Hair' and contemplate a little before opening your mouth so quickly to judge. – Zendaya Coleman'.

By the next morning, everyone was talking about Zendaya, and *The Washington Post* was asking the question the world wanted an answer to. 'Who is Zendaya?' DuVernay responded to the young star via Twitter, tweeting, 'You're beautiful, Queen. We bless the ignorant and wish them well. Onward. xo.'

In an interview on *Good Morning America*, Zendaya revealed that she had thought long and hard before posting. 'I had to stop myself from being ignorant and being a kid … I had to really take my time and think about what my parents taught me, which is [that] the most important things in the world are your voice and your knowledge, being that they're both educators. So, I sat in my room and I used both of those things. There is a fine line between what is funny and disrespectful.'

A mortified Rancic also took to Twitter to apologize. But the damage had been done. 'I'm sorry I offended you and others,' she tweeted. 'I was referring to a bohemian chic look. Had

NOTHING to do with race and NEVER would!!!' She followed that up by issuing an apology on air saying, 'As you know, *Fashion Police* is a show that pokes fun at celebrities in good spirit, but I do realize that something I said last night did cross the line. I just want everyone to know that I didn't intend to hurt anybody, but I have learned it's not my intent that matters. It's the result. And the result is people are offended, including Zendaya, and that is not okay. Therefore, I want to say to Zendaya, and anyone else out there that I hurt, that I'm so sincerely sorry. This really has been a learning experience for me. I learned a lot today and this incident has taught me to be a lot more aware of cliches and stereotypes, and how much damage they can do. And that I am responsible, as we all are, to not perpetuate them further.'

Zendaya graciously accepted the apology, with a cleverly worded caveat of: 'I'm glad it was a learning experience for you and for the network.' She later elaborated in an interview with *Complex* magazine. 'It was a learning experience for myself and for everyone who read it. A lot of people don't realize that hair is a big thing for a lot of people, not just African-American women. It's something to be aware of and to be cautious of. So, it was something that I really felt like I should speak on.'

Zendaya added that so many women, of all races, had come up to her and made comments like, 'I really love what you said,' or, 'I had my daughter read that.' Her young nephews and nieces had also been on her mind when she'd tweeted the response. One day they would have Twitter and Instagram, and now she would be able to advise them how to react if ever they came up against outdated racial stereotypes. A relative unknown,

Zendaya was now steering a national dialogue about race with intelligence, poise and tact. Hundreds of women from across the USA sent her images of themselves wearing locs: something empowering and overwhelmingly positive. Zendaya's response had opened up a dialogue, allowing people to talk about things that made them feel uncomfortable. It was a massive moment not just for her but for all women of colour. But she knew there was still a long way to go.

Asked what he made of the way his daughter handled the situation, Kazembe Coleman points to his cheek. 'My allergies acted up,' he joked. 'I was overwhelmed with pride.'

As well he might be. It was Zendaya rather than the victors at the Academy Awards who became the story. The Oscars? Forget it! All anyone wanted to talk about was Zendaya and her measured, mature response to the incident. The Disney kid from Oakland was all over the media – and for all the right reasons. Her stylist Law Roach bestowed her with the nickname 'Zoprah'.

Zendaya herself would look back at that early career moment while speaking to *W* magazine several years later. She described it as a turning point for not just her own career, but for Hollywood as a whole, in determining what kind of commentary and remarks should not and could not be tolerated towards actors of colour. 'That's how change happens,' she said. 'And it made me think, how could I always have a lasting impact on what people saw and associated with people of colour?'

'Loc-gate' resulted in the creation of a one-off Barbie doll 'Shero'. She was created especially for Zendaya and was dressed in a white column gown with her hair in locs. According to the manufacturers Mattel, to be considered for 'Shero' status, a woman needed to have broken boundaries, inspired girls and played with Barbies as a girl herself. Zendaya had certainly broken down boundaries and inspired people of all ages by encouraging them to stand up for themselves. She later hosted the *Barbie: Rock 'N Royals Concert Experience*, an event benefiting VH1 Save The Music Foundation. The event encouraged kids to 'Raise Their Voices' in a first-of-its-kind experience including up-and-coming musical and dance acts, meet and greets with Zendaya, and a rock star zone where kids could jam out on guitars, drums, trumpets and more. The brand activated nine concert experiences across the globe with different local hosts encouraging kids to raise their voices through the arts. Mattel also set about introducing more diversity into their 'Fashionistas' line, including twenty-three new dolls, featuring eight skin tones, fourteen different sculpts, eighteen eye colours and twenty-three different hair colours. Zendaya took her position as role model seriously. It was very important for her to set an example for future generations, and she was proud and honoured to be regarded in this way. But she was neither patronizing nor big-headed about it. And nor was there any pretence.

'If you pretend to be a role, one day that role is going to break,' she told *TIME* magazine in 2015. 'You are going to want to be yourself, and people are going to be really disappointed finding out you're not who you've been living your life to be. Just keep it real and be yourself.'

She elaborated on the theme in a chat with HuffPost that same year.

'I think it's a responsibility, but like Tupac Shakur, "I'm a real model," which means: I'm not pretending to be something that I'm not, because like he said, people are going to be disappointed when they find out who you are, because it's not going to be what you presented to the world,' she said. 'So just keep it real. I'm a good kid and that's all.'

Zendaya was certainly keeping it real when she did a modelling session for the cover of *Modeliste* magazine in September 2015. She looked stunning, as always, but she wasn't happy when she realized the photos had been heavily touched up. Her already svelte nineteen-year-old hips and torso had been manipulated to make her look even slimmer. Many stars would have let it go. Not Zendaya.

'These are the things that make women self-conscious, that create the unrealistic ideals of beauty that we have,' she wrote on Instagram. 'Anyone who knows who I am knows I stand for honest and pure self-love. So, I took it upon myself to release the real pic and I love it. Thank you @modelistemagazine for pulling down the images and fixing this retouch issue.'

The magazine pulled the photos before the issue was published but went a step further by releasing a letter from the editor, thanking their cover star for bringing attention to the issue. 'Thank You Zendaya,' it read, 'for raising a very important issue. In light of our not-yet-released November issue, with *Modeliste*'s Cover Girl, Zendaya, and the swirling controversy in regards to any retouched images, I am compelled to publicly address this situation which was brought to my attention yesterday, personally by Zendaya […] we concluded that the images had been retouched to an extent that was not acceptable and not true to the values and ideals we represent and promote in our publication. I, therefore, made the executive decision to immediately pull the issue in order to have this rectified and have the images restored to their original, natural state which will reflect the true beauty and radiance of Zendaya. We [...] specifically chose Zendaya as our Cover Model for the issue as we have a deep respect and admiration for her openness, honesty, the genuine manner in which she connects with her loyal fan base, as well as her integrity. We believe her to be an authentic and positive representative and an inspiration to women and of the values which we at *Modeliste* also hold [...] We are proud that Zendaya has taken this as an opportunity to address this situation, and create a very necessary honest and open dialogue.'

Now a prestigious fashion magazine was bowing to Zendaya's will and wisdom. By speaking out against the image retouching she won herself legions more fans and massive respect throughout the media.

'I realized that if I don't like something, I can change it,' she told *Cosmopolitan* magazine. 'If I don't feel comfortable with something, then I have a voice to say it's not cool.'

A few weeks before this incident, a project very close to Zendaya's heart – and feet – came to fruition. Collaborating with Titan Industries, she unveiled her first collection of shoes, named Daya, after her family nickname. She travelled to New York for a launch event, where she unveiled her debut collection of sixteen spring styles. In the Titan Industries' showroom, Zendaya sat down with *Footwear News* to talk shoes and her exciting new foray into the world of fashion. 'I wanted shoes that were going to speak for themselves,' she said, 'If consumers didn't know who the heck I was, which a lot of people don't, they are still going to like the shoes. I don't want people buying because they're Zendaya shoes – they are for everyone.'

The venture was a collaboration between Zendaya and her long-time stylist Law Roach. Prices ranged from an affordable $70 to $110 and included everything from stylish trainers and pointed-toe flats to 6-inch (15 cm) stilettos. Although standing a statuesque 5 feet 10 inches (178 cm) tall, Zendaya loves heels as much as anyone. She comes from a line of tall, fabulous women – her mother is 6 feet 4 inches (194 cm) tall. Her ethos was that people would comment on her being tall anyway – they even did that when she was barefoot – so she might as well be extra tall and feel fabulous about it in a gorgeous pair of heels. Law Roach was right behind her, saying her stance on this subject conveyed the message that it's okay to be tall and wear heels. It's okay to be the tallest girl in the room. More than okay, in fact.

Zendaya was, as everyone knew, in love with clothes, so why had she chosen shoes for her first foray into the world of fashion? 'Well, first of all, I'm obsessed with them,' she told *Glamour* magazine. 'But it was a good place to start because there are so many fashion categories you can get into, this felt like a more controlled environment where I could focus and get started. I don't want to give myself too much too quickly and jump into the deep end when I'm not ready.'

She added that she was inspired by the women in her family – her mother, older sisters and grown-up niece. As a girl from an ordinary home, she hadn't grown up with parents who could afford Louboutins or Jimmy Choos, and so many non-designer shoes looked and felt cheap. What Zendaya wanted to achieve with her range was stylish footwear that looked and felt luxurious but was affordable.

As 2016 dawned, there was a second series of *K.C. Undercover* in the can. However, by the end of the year Zendaya would be cast in a blockbuster feature film that would change her professional life – and ultimately her private one – forever.

Zendaya's Sheroes

An official 'shero' since 2015, Zendaya continues to be a role model for women of all shapes, sizes, creeds, colours and ages. But she has sheroes of her own, women whom she looks up to and regards as her role models. First and foremost is her mother, Claire Maree Stoermer. In an interview with Beyoncé's mother, Tina Knowles-Lawson, on her Instagram show *Talks with Mama Tina* in 2021, Zendaya couldn't praise Claire highly enough.

'My mom is a shero to me. She brought me into the world for a start. I'm so grateful for my mother. I learned so much from her. I think often she doesn't even know the lessons that she's teaching. I think I learned so much just watching her exist and be who she is.'

For Zendaya, the predominant life lesson she learned from Claire was selflessness. She witnessed how her mother taught in underprivileged communities for twenty years, working tirelessly to enable her students to have experiences such as outdoor science camp. For many former students, they felt that if it hadn't been for Ms Stoermer, their lives would have been rudderless. Claire had gone above and beyond what was required of a teacher, instinctively knowing that an inspiring educator was capable of changing his or her students' lives.

It goes without saying that Zendaya herself was a recipient of her mother's selflessness. After all, in 2010, Claire had been willing to stay in Oakland and work two jobs to keep the family financially afloat while Zendaya and Kazembe relocated to Los Angles to get young Zendaya's career off the ground. It was also from Claire that Zendaya learned not to be profligate with her money once she started earning big bucks.

As always, she did her homework before the in-person audition. The character was fifteen years old. Fifteen, hmm … at fifteen, Zendaya hadn't been allowed to wear make-up to school, so she decided to attend the initial audition barefaced. It was Zendaya's shape-shifter ability – looking uber glam one minute and totally natural the next – that first attracted and intrigued *Spider-Man* director Jon Watts. He found her to be an amazingly technical actor, plus she added her own flourishes, such as the barefaced hack and carrying around a mug of strange herbal tea, which she instinctively felt the character she was up for would do. The 'girl in movie' would turn out to be Michelle Jones-Watson, more commonly known as MJ, and a modern take on Mary Jane 'MJ' Watson, who had featured as Spidey's recurring love interest in the original comic books. However, this MJ was very different. Whereas the comic book MJ had been a flamboyant, slightly flaky party animal, Michelle was super smart, quirky, outspoken, bookish, sarcastic and more concerned with activism than boys. Not unlike Zendaya in certain ways, then. She had to perform a 'chemistry read' with British actor Tom Holland, who was playing Peter Parker, and there was an awkward moment when they met. He went to shake her hand, while Zendaya pulled him in for a hug. She was also said to be concerned that she was taller than Tom, who is 5 feet 8 inches (173 cm) tall. How would that pan out in romantic scenes or when, as Spidey, he had to rescue her? But as soon as they started acting opposite each other there was a clear connection, a definite dynamism, between them. However, Zendaya was still far from convinced she would land the role.

'A lot of time, the thought process of an actor of color is "I'm going to go and give it my best shot, but they are probably not going to go with an actor of color for this,"' she told 8 Days showbiz website. 'I didn't know they were going to switch up the characters and really cast the best people for the roles instead of what's most like the comic book.'

And the best person for the role of this new MJ was Zendaya. The fact that the film-makers were embracing diversity was one of the coolest things about it for her. It wasn't a big part, true, but it was a good one. As Zendaya had anticipated, there was controversy over the casting. This centred upon the fact that Zendaya, a mixed-race actress, would be portraying the comic book's pale-skinned, red-haired MJ Watson. Media outlets defended Zendaya over the issue on social media, along with the *Guardians of the Galaxy* director James Gunn and Mary Jane co-creator Stan Lee. But still, there were some old-school Spider-Man purists who weren't happy. One Twitter user tweeted, 'Since Mary Jane is being played by a Black woman, can Martin Luther King be played by a White man in a next movie about him?'

Zendaya responded to this backlash in an interview with *The Hollywood Reporter* magazine, saying: 'Of course there's going to be outrage over that because for some reason some people just aren't ready. I'm like, "I don't know what America you live in, but from what I see when I walk outside my streets of New York right now, I see lots of diversity and I see the real world and it's beautiful, and that's what should be reflected and that's what is reflected so you're just going to have to get over it."' Touché!

She had made her feelings known on this topic before, telling *Hunger* magazine in 2015 that, 'America is such a melting pot – everyone's from everywhere. The only people who are native are Native Americans. So, everyone's an immigrant. I have pride in that I'm an African American. I think when you develop pride in where you're from then you have more respect and understanding in terms of where other people are from also.'

Not only was Zendaya perfect for the role of MJ, but it was

also an inspired move by the makers of the film to cast her. Throughout her career, she had brought aspirational, strong characters of colour into the world of children's television, and in doing so she had become a kind of beacon of hope for her then-41-million Instagram followers. She was something of a superhero herself. On more than one occasion, she was mobbed during filming while shooting scenes for the movie in Atlanta, with many fans in tears to actually see their 'shero' in the flesh. And such was the Zendaya–Tom chemistry on-screen, there were rumours that they were in a relationship off-screen as well – something both categorically denied. They had become great friends but that was all. While this *was* true back in 2016 and 2017, it wouldn't always be the case! Meanwhile, Zendaya totally relished the process of starring in a mainstream movie, and the shoot was a happy one.

'We have a great group of people, a great cast,' she told Flicks and the City Clips website from the *Spider-Man* set, mid-filming. 'Like, we hang out all the time. It's not forced – it's not like "Hey you guys, get along with each other." Everybody is, in a weird way, very similar to their characters.'

Next up for Zendaya was another blockbuster: *The Greatest Showman*. It was based on the story of real-life entertainer and showman P. T. Barnum and his Barnum and Bailey Circus in the late nineteenth and early twentieth centuries. She had first heard about the film two years earlier when she was introduced to the director, Michael Gracey, by the people at Fox. He was greatly impressed by Zendaya, telling her she would be perfect for the character of Anne Wheeler, a dazzlingly talented young trapeze artist who had been specifically invented for the film. Gracey had played her footage of Hugh Jackman – the Australian star who would play Barnum – singing some of the numbers from the production, and Zendaya immediately wanted in. Knowing that she'd have to sing in the audition, and once again thinking ahead, she asked to be given the songs she would be singing in the film – if she got the part, that is – in advance, hoping to record them and impress Gracey. She recorded her part of 'Rewrite the Stars', the number that would be her duet with her movie love interest, played by Zac Efron, in her home studio in the garage at the Echo Park family home. When she later auditioned, she played the recording to Gracey and Efron. They were deeply impressed by both her performance and the thought and preparation that had gone into it, but Zendaya still wasn't sure the part was hers until Zac, also a former Disney kid, spelled it out to her. Throughout the audition, unbeknown to Zendaya, Gracey had continually given Zac impressed glances. He then asked her to hang out with Zac and himself. Zac presumed that this would have given Zendaya the nod that she'd landed the role. It hadn't!

Anne Wheeler was a complex character. Beautiful and talented, as an African American she was deeply affected by the racism endemic in nineteenth-century American culture. She felt like an outsider, and this hampered her relationship with Zac's fictional character, businessman Philip Carlyle. The two fall in love as soon as they lay eyes on each other, but Carlyle and Anne had to deal with disapproving families as well as a racist American society. Serious acting was required to convey these issues in addition to having to sing and, well, trapeze. Playing a circus performer of some repute, Zendaya would need to trapeze like a pro – in addition to twirling and whirling around in mid-air with Zac. Cue intense preparation: Zendaya and Zac rehearsed every number in the film in great detail before they even started shooting, as director Gracey wanted to film everything almost as if they were doing a real Broadway show. He also wanted Zendaya to do as much of the trapeze work as possible herself rather than using a stunt double. This saw her embarking on intense, regular workouts to gain upper body strength, develop more muscular arms and just generally become as strong and toned as possible. Working out every day was a new and not altogether pleasant experience for Zendaya. She'd never been a gym bunny. However, the hard work paid off. She was soon strong enough to pull herself up, backwards and forwards. It was at this point that the trapeze training properly commenced. Instructed by her trapeze trainers, Zendaya initially practised on a specific 'rig', which she soon became familiar with. There was also a reassuring safety net in situ, so she felt she was in her comfort zone. She'd got this! But when the time came to try out the real rig on the real set … scary! The rig was 15 feet (5 m) taller than the practice one, plus the net was missing. Zendaya had serious doubts that she'd be able to pull it off. It's maybe thanks to Hugh Jackman that she did.

'Right before I went out to try it for the first time, Hugh said to me: "Zendaya, you are a badass,"' she told the New Paper. 'That was all I needed – that encouragement from him. I got started and I felt great, and I did not have that fear anymore. My body went through a lot – bruises and soreness – but I did not even feel it when I was in the air.'

Her 'up-in-the-air' set pieces with Zac were yet another challenge. Zendaya found him to be a very supportive partner, which would be of vital importance, seeing that at times they'd be harnessed together with Zac having to take her weight. There was a certain sweetness and romance to their on-screen partnership, with Zac later revealing to Filmweb that of all the on-screen kisses he'd ever had to do, his smooch with Zendaya was *numero uno*.

'This might be my favorite kiss, I think ever,' he said. 'Just because at this point for these characters, it's so built up, the tension between them is so strong, and literally, just a glance between them is electric.'

It was good for Zendaya, too, although admittedly her then-experience of screen kisses was somewhat limited. She also told Filmweb, 'When you're into a character, the whole time, they're not allowed to as much as touch, talk, speak, have a moment between each other; so every moment, even if they're just touching, is incredibly special.'

Director Michael Gracey was blown away with Zendaya, proclaiming that she was Hollywood's greatest star in the making. She could act, she could trapeze(!) and she sang like an angel. She would go on to appear on three tracks of the film's soundtrack, including 'Rewrite the Stars', which would be nominated for an Oscar in 2018.

'I would ask her to do the craziest things,' Gracey related to the New Paper. 'When she was swinging around the rig with a camera out in front of her, I would say, "Just catch this hat and then throw it on this word of the song," and she would smile and do it all so effortlessly. For someone so young, she has an amazing commitment to her work.'

Hugh Jackman, too, could not praise her highly enough. 'She's a pure natural. She is unbelievably respectful to everyone she works with. Incredibly professional. This really hasn't happened very often in my life – to work with someone where it's blindingly obvious that she is going to be, if she wants it, the biggest star of her generation. And that could be in music or dance or acting – whatever she wants.'

Unsurprisingly Zendaya was busy, busy, busy. The past year had been a whirlwind. In addition to making two big, potentially blockbuster films, squeezing in a season of K.C. Undercover for Disney, and, oh, appearing in the music video for the song 'Versace on the Floor' by Bruno Mars, she had also somehow found the time to launch a clothing brand. With Law Roach by her side every step of the (run)way, 'Daya by Zendaya' (a sequel to her footwear line) comprised a carefully curated selection of tops, bottoms, dresses, jumpsuits and outerwear that was super stylish but affordable, with the most expensive garment retailing at $158. As well as price, it was also important to Zendaya to be as inclusive as possible, and the range was sized from US 0 to 22.

'I didn't want anyone to feel alienated, excluded, or feel like they weren't a part of this,' Zendaya told Refinery29. 'I want my mom to be able to wear my stuff. I want my older sister to be able to wear my stuff. I want thick women, tall women, skinny women to wear my stuff.'

Another conscious decision made by Zendaya and Law was to include many gender-neutral options, in an attempt to override binary fashion rules. There *were* no rules where style was concerned. Zendaya didn't care how the public wore her clothes. The only thing that mattered was feeling good about yourself. When she was included in *Forbes* magazine's prestigious 'Forbes 30 Under 30' for her success and influencer power as an actress and performer, and also as a force to be reckoned with in the fashion world, she must have felt very good indeed.

Having left her teenage years behind as she turned twenty in September 2016, much was afoot in Zendaya's non-work life. Her father, Kazembe, began to take more of a back seat in the running of her career. He had tried to carry on working for her once his daughter had taken charge of her own business matters, around the time of her twentieth birthday, but he found it challenging to have the roles reversed with his baby girl telling him what to do. There were no bad feelings – Kazembe had always known this moment would come. But it seemed to mark a turning point in all their lives. In August 2016, Claire Stoermer had filed divorce papers against Kazembe Ajamu Coleman, citing irreconcilable differences. She did not ask for spousal support. Zendaya's fans may have been shocked at this news, but Zendaya was not. 'My parents ain't been together for a long time – y'all didn't know cause we private, they still homies,' she tweeted, accompanied by a recent photo of the three of them posing happily together.

What wasn't so happy was the online abuse Claire and Kazembe were subjected to, with online trolls calling them both ugly. 'First I'm gonna pray for you,' Zendaya tweeted back. 'While you're so concerned about what my parents look like, please know that these are two of the most selfless people in the world. Please, log out, go to school, hug a teacher and read a textbook. And while you're at it, go look in the mirror and know that you too are beautiful, because such hateful things only stem from internal struggles. Bless you.' Another measured, beautifully worded response.

As 2017 dawned, Zendaya revealed to *Vogue* that throughout most of 2016, she'd secretly been recovering from a big break-up with her boyfriend of the past four years – presumably Trevor Jackson, who had given her a dog, named Noon, as a Christmas gift in December 2015. A few months later, they were no longer an item, leaving Zendaya heartbroken but not ready to talk about it. She, also, was 'private'. But once time passed and heartache healed, she was ready. In a social media post called 'How I Survived a Broken Heart', Zendaya opened up about what helped get her through the tough times post break-up, recommending the benefits of being more open, being willing to try new things and having a good old clear-out of messages, photos and mementos.

'I got rid of old text messages, pictures and their clothing I still had. You don't hang on to old band-aids. Throw that in the trash!' she recommended. 'You have to get rid of everything associated with them. It's best to get rid of their number. Or if you can't quite let go, at least change the title of their name in your phone.'

She closed by saying that although it had been her first love and it hadn't ended well, she knew she was on the road to recovery when her first thought was no longer, 'What did I do wrong?' but 'That was the dumbest decision of your life.'

On the *Ellen Show* in March 2016, Zendaya had extolled the virtues of still living at home. In early 2017, however, she moved from the family home in Echo Park into a five-bedroom, five-bathroom, three balcony, 4,155 square foot (386 m²) Mediterranean-style house complete with gourmet chef kitchen, swimming pool, outdoor spa and an expansive patio area, which she bought for $1.4 million dollars in the Northridge neighbourhood of Los Angeles. She filmed a video of the house and duly posted on social media, unable to believe that this gorgeous property was now hers. She particularly loved the fairy-tale main staircase.

'Guys, I've always wanted stairs like this like literally since I was a little girl,' she posted. 'Because you know, I'm from Oakland, humble beginnings, I have two parents as teachers so I've never lived in a two-story house or a house with air conditioning or a house with a pool so this is crazy. I have a staircase, it's like the Cinderella spiral staircase. I've never lived in a house this beautiful. I appreciate everything so much more because everything I have has been worked for.'

Not that she lived there alone. She told *Harper's Bazaar* that she didn't like being in a big house by herself and that she loved having people around her. She shared the space with one of her sisters, a niece, some cousins, her assistant Darnell Apping and her dog Noon – it was a full house. Darnell had come into her life thanks to *K.C. Undercover*. He had been her body double on the show and the two formed an immediate bond, with Zendaya calling him her 'brother'. He certainly went above and beyond his brotherly duties. The night before New York's prestigious Met Gala in May 2017, Zendaya suddenly developed an ugly rash on her face and back. Darnell urged her to go to an emergency room (ER) at a hospital to have it checked. Zendaya was reluctant. She'd feel like a total diva sweeping in there with her security detail while medics were dealing with real sickness, diseases and emergencies. But finally, Darnell convinced her to go. It turned out that she was having an allergic reaction to an antibiotic she was taking for a throat infection. She immediately stopped taking it and the doctors gave her new medicine to help clear up the rash, just in time for the Gala. The theme was Comme des Garçons, but Zendaya chose not to follow it, which made her immediately stand out. She wore a show-stopping Dolce & Gabbana ball gown in bright yellow, orange and blue fabric adorned with a pattern of tropical parrots. Pairing the dress with a striking Afro hairdo and orange-red lipstick, it was a picture-perfect look that totally stole the show at this, her third Met Gala. Posting the story of an eventful 24 hours on Instagram, she ended it with a grateful shout-out to her saviours, posting that 'the real heroes of the world work at the ER in New York, at 11-something at night.'

Spider-Man: Homecoming was released in June 2017 in the USA and worldwide in July. As usual, Zendaya set the red carpet alight at the premiere in Los Angeles. This was an event she had absolutely every right to attend, and she had turned up the heat, wearing a hot pink Ralph & Russo gown with a dangerously high slit, revealing nearly her entire leg. The gown even had a miniature cape that trailed behind it – especially fitting for the premiere of a superhero movie. She paired the bold dress with matching pink heels and opted for natural-looking make-up and softly waved hair. The film was a smash hit, which would go on to gross more than $630 million worldwide, and the reviews for Zendaya's short appearance were glowing, proving that she was that rare beast – a child star with mainstream crossover appeal. In August 2017, she won the best movie actress gong for playing MJ at the Teen Choice Awards. The year also saw her become the cover girl for Cover Girl cosmetics, following in the illustrious footsteps of Tyra Banks and Queen Latifah.

The Greatest Showman was released in late December 2017. The film met with mixed reception, although it would go on to become the third-highest-grossing live-action musical ever released. *Variety* praised Zendaya's chemistry with Zac Efron, writing that she brought 'a touching sensitivity to her handful of scenes'. It goes without saying that she nailed her red carpet looks at the various premieres that took place in locations around the globe. In Sydney, Australia, she had jaws dropping as she modelled a stunning Moschino butterfly-themed dress, which she would later refer to as one of her all-time favourite looks. In Mexico City, she rocked slim-fitting black trousers with a scarlet brocade dinner jacket and heels. And at the New York premiere, aboard the *Queen Mary 2* ocean liner anchored in New York Harbor in Brooklyn, she looked majestically beautiful in a strapless black lace dress, cut to reveal a frothy scarlet, floor-length petticoat.

As 2018 dawned, Zendaya was on the crest of a wave.

Fairy Dog Mother

It is said to be a dog's life and Noon Coleman is one pooch most definitely to be envied. The six-year-old jet black miniature schnauzer is without doubt one of the loves of Zendaya's life. She calls herself his 'mom' and refers to him as her beloved son. He has his own Instagram account with 27,000 followers on which 'he' makes announcements such as: 'I am the beloved son of the great Zendaya Maree. I like long naps w/ treats as a reward. Getting on my uncle Darnell's last nerve is what I'm best at'. Speaking to Australia's *Total Girl* magazine, Zendaya spoke of how much she loves him, saying that while it is usually dogs who crave attention from their owners, it was she who craved more attention from him.

Noon came into Zendaya's life at Christmastime in 2015 and was said to be a gift from her then-boyfriend, Trevor Jackson. A few months earlier, Zendaya had been left heartbroken when her childhood pet, Midnight, a giant schnauzer, had passed away.

'My baby went to heaven today,' she posted on her Instagram page. 'Thank you for being one of the most loyal men in my life, for loving me unconditionally and for cuddling me whenever I needed. I don't know if you ever understood me when I told you but I love you more than you'll ever know. We've been together since I was 8 and I'm not really sure how to get use to a house without your cute paws clinking around ... but thank you for every second of love you gave us.'

She couldn't contain her joy when the new puppy arrived in her life. 'Most of you know I lost my baby Midnight a while ago, and I thought I could never love another pet again ... until this little angel was given to me on Christmas Eve ... he's literally a mini Midnight ... he peed on my bed 3 times last night and I didn't care,' she wrote. 'I mean look at that face! What a beautiful gift ... right when I needed it the most. I'm so thankful for this little man.'

She named him Noon as it seemed so perfect after Midnight. She was smitten with her new dog from the start, letting him fall asleep in her arms and then not moving for fear of waking him up. Her dog's postings, accompanied by phrases like 'I miss home', sat alongside posts in which they can be seen huddled together – they were always together. There wasn't, and never has been, any regular routine-type doggy day care for this boy while Zendaya works. Right from the start, he was a celebrity dog, going with her everywhere. Noon's always been a set dog, travelling – often by private jet no less – wherever in the world Zendaya happens to be going. But this kind of high-octane, uber-pedigree lifestyle can bring its own problems for any canine. Noon, although in close proximity to Zendaya while she was working, often spent long hours of downtime alone in her trailer while she was filming. These periods would be interrupted by instances of intensified excitement and affection when mother and son were briefly reunited. It was something of an emotional roller coaster for Noon. Walking the dog meant a quick circumnavigation of the film lot rather than a lengthy hike or anonymous wander around a public park. The result? Noon's behaviour wasn't all that it should be. He was overexcited when he encountered people, and he could also be aggressive and has growled at babies and other dogs.

In 2017, Cesar Millan, the host of *Dog Whisperer* and *Dog Nation*, visited Noon and Zendaya at home in order to shed light on why the dog was behaving in the way he was – with the consultation being recorded by *Vogue* magazine. Millan asked Zendaya what she thought the problem was.

'His biggest problem is he doesn't spend a lot of time around other dogs, because he's constantly on-set with me,' Zendaya replied. 'When it comes to other dogs, or children, he just loses it. He tried to fight a German Shepherd once, and the German Shepherd handed it to him. He's been neutered, which has helped, but he's not the best listener. He's hyper excited but that's because he's allowed to be. I'm definitely an enabler. I'm definitely not good at telling him no. That I know.'

Cesar Millan explained than when a dog lived an unusually exciting life, like Noon, with no real rules, boundaries or limitations, the dog would behave just how Noon was behaving. And while human beings were often tolerant of an overexcited dog, other dogs most definitely were not. Noon, not used to encountering other canines, would start barking when he met any – more out of excitement than aggression – and want to immediately start playing. His would-be playmates wouldn't be impressed. They would, said Millan, be thinking it was too soon to do the play stuff before they'd barely said hello. Mutual bum sniffing came before anything else. That was how dogs became acquainted with each other.

'What you have here is a dog that is borderline hyper and a human who does affection, affection, affection,' Millan explained to Zendaya about her and Noon's relationship. 'Try to raise a kid with affection, affection, affection. What is that called? A spoiled kid.'

Zendaya conceded that the dog whisperer was right. After a short period of interacting with Millan, with the human 'dogspert' gently chastising Noon and beginning to set boundaries, the dog started to calm down. Millan then decided to introduce Noon to his own dogs, who were waiting in his car. Zendaya was nervous, worried how Noon would react, but Millan said she must hide this. The authority figure must not project fear, he said, adding that an afraid dog would not be able to trust. The upshoot was that by the end of the session, having introduced himself to Noon as a role model of authority, Millan was able to calm the dog down and oversee the mostly harmonious meetings between Zendaya's boy and firstly a Yorkshire terrier, then a pug, a Pomeranian and finally a pit bull.

'You don't have an aggressive dog,' Millan told Zendaya. 'You have a dog that needs exercise, calmness and instruction.'

Zendaya took these instructions on board and Noon, although still a celebrity, has dispensed with his diva-like behaviour. However, his mother is well aware that he's no goodie-four-paws. She has said that if he was to attend Hogwarts, he would most definitely be Slytherin.

'Slytherin all day. Noon is Voldemort,' she told IMDb, asserting that her pup shares more traits with Severus Snape than Dumbledore. 'He's more of a Snape … He'll be cold to you but he'll look out for you … He'll be cold to you and then what? Cuddle!'

FIVE

Goodbye Disney ... Hello Euphoria

'It's a scary jump but I think it was time for me to do this' – **Zendaya**
to *The New York Times* on leaving
Disney and embarking on *Euphoria*

The final episode of *K.C. Undercover* aired on the Disney Channel on 2 February 2018. Zendaya had known for almost a year that there would be no more after the third season and, after eight years at Disney, she was finally ready to break away.

It felt a little like her television career had stagnated. Now that she had starred in two big-budget films, making more *K.C.* – or any other Disney show for that matter – would have seemed like a step backwards. And at twenty-one, she could hardly be regarded as a 'kid' anymore.

'After shooting *The Greatest Showman* and *Spider-Man*, I went back to my Disney show, which is kind of like going to college and then having to go back and do the same grade over and over again,' Zendaya was later to tell *US Weekly*. 'Not that I didn't appreciate having a job. But it's like you turn a switch on and do it, and then you get turned off and go home. I wanted more.'

On the evening the final episode of *K.C. Undercover* was aired, Zendaya reflected on Twitter that this was her very last episode on the Disney Channel, which had been her showbiz home for eight years. It was the end of an era, and she thanked her fans and followers for continuing to grow with her. Going into 2018, she had decided to concentrate on acting rather than continue with a solo singing career. Still a naturally shy person, she enjoyed the anonymity of playing a part rather than having to be herself at all times – obviously, necessary for a singer. She also felt the music industry had taken a piece of her passion for music away. She felt it had sucked her dry and that wasn't what she wanted anymore.

The new year saw her voicing characters in the animated films *Duck Duck Goose* and *Smallfoot*. In the former production, she played a duckling who gets separated from her flock, but her role in the musical animation *Smallfoot* is more complex.

The film's narrative explores the isolated life of yetis (a yeti is also known as an abominable snowman, bigfoot or sasquatch), as their world is turned upside down by the discovery of human beings – and vice versa. The film explores themes of standing up for what you believe in and staying true to yourself. These are themes that have obviously resonated with Zendaya, who voiced a yeti character called Meechee in the film.

'I like to remind myself that my gut instinct is always the best one,' she told *Glamour* magazine. 'I think often we let too many voices get into our head and too much doubt, too much fear. I sometimes think you should just listen to that immediate gut reaction to something – it's usually the right feeling to trust. You should just try to follow that and if it doesn't feel all the way right then don't do it.'

An added bonus for Zendaya was getting to sing 'Wonderful Life' in the film – a song about exploring life's curiosities and the wonders of it all. Animated films aside, there was also talk of Zendaya starring in *A White Lie,* the film adaption of Karin Tanabe's 2016 book, *The Gilded Years*. Set in the 1890s, Zendaya was said to be in talks to portray the main character, Anita Hemmings, who was the first African-American woman to graduate from Vassar College. However, the production never got off the ground.

By mid-2018, without any Disney safety net to catch her, Zendaya found herself feeling concerned about her future career – something she hadn't need to worry about for a decade. Historically, the post-Disney transition hasn't always been easy for young artists to navigate. Many former stars have alluded to the fact that Disney expected its actors to have a squeaky-clean image well into their teens and twenties, which could make the artists feel like forever-children which, in turn, can make it harder to land adult roles later on. Zendaya's former *Shake It Up* co-star, Bella Thorne, said that she was expected to speak in a higher pitch to seem younger than she was, and Selena Gomez similarly noted that working for the network often left her feeling immense pressure to be 'the good girl'.

In Zendaya's next role, she would be anything but the good girl. In looking for an all-absorbing new project, she hankered after the same feeling she'd experienced with both *Spider-Man: Homecoming* and *The Greatest Showman.* The sense that she just *had* to do it, no matter what. She didn't want to take a job just because she needed a job. She wanted a role in a project that she had an all-encompassing passion for, something that she could really believe in. The gods must have read her thoughts. She received a call from her manager about a project that HBO was developing called *Euphoria*. This was an adaptation of an Israeli 2012 teen soap of the same name – but rather darker. HBO's version was a story of drugs, sex, identity, trauma, social media, love and friendship, narrated by a lying, drug-addicted seventeen-year-old girl named Ruby 'Rue' Bennett. Zendaya wanted to play Rue. Very badly. While there was little in the role that she could personally identify with – she'd never touched drink nor drugs and was a self-confessed bad liar – Zendaya knew she'd be miserable if she wasn't part of this extraordinary, groundbreaking new series.

'I fell in love with who Rue was,' Zendaya recalled to *Paper* magazine. 'It felt special because I don't like to read scripts, and for me to read through it faster than anything I've ever read before, obviously I connected with it somehow.'

This role would be, by far, Zendaya's grittiest to date. Rue was inspired by *Euphoria* creator and writer Sam Levinson's own youth, which had been deeply troubled due to his obsessive drug use. This gave the show a deeply personal insight in addition to a much-needed layer of authenticity and urgency. Levinson had also taken inspiration from the likes of earlier gritty television series such as *Kids* and *Skins*, while also tackling contemporary realities such as active-shooter drills and revenge porn.

'It's the story of how kids navigate the world today,' he told HBO. 'And it's from their perspective. There is an incredible amount of judgement shown towards young people for being on social media. It's always something that's perceived as a narcissistic pursuit but the world is changing month by month. It asks, "How do we create empathy for this generation from an older generation?"'

Levinson found writing about his own battles with addiction therapeutic, and he saw something in Zendaya that made him feel she'd be perfect as Rue – even though she had no life experiences of the issues herself. When he told Zendaya that she'd been on his mood board for the project, she hadn't believed him.

'There's no way he saw anything I did in the past and thought, "Hmm, that girl could potentially play me,"' Zendaya told *Paper* magazine in the same interview. 'The character Rue is basically him and his life experiences. I felt so worried about proving myself. It was very scary.'

In addition to Zendaya's perfectionist streak coming to the fore – the innate trait of hers that made her want to make a success of everything she did – there was extra pressure because she was a Disney alumnus. She knew people would be expecting her to fail. There was a lot for her to prove. However, Levinson was prepared to take a punt on Zendaya – he didn't see her casting as being risky. Gut instinct told him she was perfect to play Rue – and he was right. While watching Zendaya play the role, he said it felt very real and that it was, in many ways, like watching himself as a seventeen year old. It was like he was seeing a version of himself navigating the world at a young age, but as if he was observing it from a parental perspective. It was strange and yet deeply moving. There was a reason Zendaya had featured on his mood board for the show. He knew she could vacillate between seeming extremely tough and extremely vulnerable. It was all in her face. She could flip on a coin, and this ability of hers was just what was needed for Rue, who had to show her moods being a mix of madness and sweetness. He instinctively felt Zendaya could do this. She was reassured by his faith in her. Whenever she voiced a concern, he'd reply, 'Yo, Z, I'm not worried about you'.

Zendaya prepared for the role by speaking with and learning extensively from Levinson. She knew how important it was to her portrayal of Rue to glean as much information and feeling as possible from the person who had created the character. Who had lived the character. The role was an absolute gift for Zendaya and just what she needed at this stage of her career.

'I just got so lucky to meet him and that he saw something in me that I could translate that or trust me with that much of his life,' she told HBO. She went on say that she had a connection with Rue, that she felt the character was a version of Zendaya herself but one who lived in different circumstances and had made different choices. Rue was, at heart, a good person, but she just didn't know it. There was an innocence and a vulnerability to her that reminded you that she was a human first and an addict second.

There's no doubt that Zendaya was a talented actress, but realistically, how could she get inside the head of a broken character like Rue when she had absolutely no real-life experience of Rue's problems? Talking at length with Levinson and understanding that Rue was a version of him was one thing, but still. It turned out that the production team on *Euphoria* was also worried this could be an issue. Jennifer Venditti, *Euphoria*'s casting director, revealed to *Variety* in August 2022 that the part had nearly gone to a relative newcomer who identified more personally with Rue's struggles.

'There was a young woman who had been street scouted by my team who was a magical person and had a similar trajectory as Rue and had come around to the other side,' said Venditti. 'But with a TV show, it can be many years of work. We all loved her, but when we went through the rigor of the process, we didn't know if she could handle what it would take in terms of stamina.'

Venditti had arranged for that young woman to work with an acting coach, but ultimately she (and Levinson, of course) felt the unknown wasn't right for the role. Besides, Zendaya was always the first choice. While she had none of the life experiences of Rue, Zendaya was, according to the casting director, 'able to dig into her toolbox and access it in such a beautiful way.'

On the first day on-set, Zendaya was absolutely terrified by what she'd taken on. When in doubt, she always consulted Levinson, who would talk her through it. She was usually concerned that her performance wasn't authentic enough but, in fact, Levinson was blown away by her.

'She and I will be talking about a scene, and I'll tell her about something that happened to me,' he revealed to *Vogue*, 'and then when we start filming, she interprets what I've said in this totally unexpected, sometimes even frightening way. I'm not sure Zendaya's giving herself enough credit.'

Nowhere was this 'totally unexpected, sometimes even frightening way' better illustrated than in the harrowing fight between Rue and her mother in the second episode of the first series. To briefly recap, in the first episode we meet Rue as she gets back from rehab, where she's spent the summer following a drug overdose. However, she has no intention of staying clean, and she fakes a drug test by using her friend's urine to show her mother otherwise. Rue's continued issues with drugs causes a build-up of tension in her family, which leads to a particularly graphic fight between Rue and her mother, Leslie, played by the actress Nika King. The fight wasn't scripted – there was just a single line of stage direction, 'Rue and her mom have a fight'.

'So, I'm thinking, OK, I'll slam the door, or whatever, but this isn't what Sam had in mind,' Zendaya explained to Refinery29.

'He wanted us to improvise the scene. He said, "I want you guys to go at one another's necks. Just go, as hard as you want to go. If she goes hard, you go harder."'

Being a very calm person who neither argued, screamed nor yelled profanities at anyone – no matter how angry she might feel – this was tough for Zendaya. However, she used her skills to put herself in that kind of situation and say and do those things. It was an extremely convincing performance – but she felt lightheaded and nauseous as a result. The role was asking her to give more of herself than she had ever done before. With such intense scenes, the cast bonded very quickly; it included Jacob Elordi as the popular jock Nate Jacobs, Hunter Schafer as the trans girl Jules who quickly befriends Rue after moving to town, Storm Reid as Rue's younger sister Gia and Sydney Sweeney as Cassie.

'I think everybody in this cast feels so connected because at some point we've all had to be so vulnerable in front of each other,' Zendaya told the *Entertainment Weekly* magazine. 'Some people have had to be literally naked in front of each other, so you build this bond and this trust and this support system.'

The pilot of *Euphoria* aired on HBO in June 2019. The cinematography was blotchily inky with camera angles that were occasionally distorted and warped to recreate an almost drug trip-like sense of disorientation. The pace was incredibly fast, with over a hundred short scenes per episode – reflecting the short attention spans of people constantly on their smartphones. Before it went to air, Zendaya warned that *Euphoria* was most definitely not *K.C. Undercover*. It was drugs, booze, erect penises, apps, mental health issues, loving sex, cruel sex and nude pics … and, she added, episode one was perhaps the least explicit of the rest of the series. It was real, it was graphically raw, it was provoking and polarizing. It wasn't an easy watch. Neither was it a political statement. The aim was for it to be storytelling that allowed the viewers to think, connect and feel however they chose to feel about it. It was up to each member of the audience to react in a way that felt natural to them. But on issues of mental health, Zendaya was particularly vocal: 'I think definitely there's been, at least amongst my peers, a certain [emphasis] on not just mental health but self-care and opening up to other experiences,' she told *Paper* magazine. 'That, in turn, makes you feel like you're not alone if you are dealing with it. It makes you feel heard and not so isolated.'

Zendaya was in no doubt that playing Rue was a game-changer for her. The critics agreed. 'The former Disney star Zendaya is reinvented as the self-destructive, self-loathing Rue, in what is a truly astonishing, mesmerizing performance, upending every expectation of what she could do,' wrote *The Guardian*.

Although her head had been filled with all things *Euphoria*, by February 2018, Zendaya had been slated to return for the next Spider-Man film, *Spider-Man: Far From Home*, reprising her role as MJ Watson. Filming started in London in early July with MJ, much to Zendaya's delight, remaining very much her own person rather than the superhero's passive love interest. For Zendaya, it was important that all kinds of women were represented on-screen – including those like the unique MJ.

'I didn't want her to have to change to be the love interest, or to have to become a different person for Peter to see anything in her,' she told *Entertainment Weekly*. 'And I think the cool part is that in this he likes her for all of her quirks and the weird things she's into, the things that her whole life have made her a little bit of a loner. I think he's a little bit of a loner too, and that's why they find that connection.'

In addition to her acting career, Zendaya somehow also found time to spend considerable periods wearing her fashionista hat. For the 2018 Oscars (Hollywood's biggest red carpet event of the year) she wore a draped one-sleeved couture chiffon goddess gown with all-over gathering by Giambattista Valli, in a hue of deepest chocolate brown. Law Roach had spotted the dress on the label's spring 2018 haute couture runway and, thanks to his persistence, he was given up-to-the-wire permission to dress Zendaya in it. The end result made her look like a Grecian goddess. The stunningly elegant look was accented with diamond jewels from the Bulgari Heritage collection and Brian Atwood sandals. The consensus was that Zendaya emerged as one of the best dressed of the evening. It was a fitting return for Zendaya as this was her first Academy Awards since 2015 (when she had, of course, worn the white satin Westwood column dress and her hair in locs).

She wowed yet again at the 2018 Met Gala a few months later. The year's theme, 'Heavenly Bodies: Fashion and the Catholic Imagination', was interpreted in a variety of unique ways, but Zendaya, at Law's suggestion, decided to channel Joan of Arc in a Versace gown. This was a diplomatic move, as Donatella Versace (along with Amal Clooney and Rihanna) was honorary chair for the evening. Zendaya's sparkling silver dress was made to look like armour, yet it managed to look sexy at the same time, complete with a thigh-high slit and multiple cut-outs. She accessorized this vision with platform heels and Tiffany & Co. jewellery.

The idea that Zendaya should dress as the medieval saint had come to Law in a dream: 'When I knew the theme and Versace, we started the conversation, there were a lot of sketches from Versace and I started thinking about strong women who had a connection to religion,' he told *Women's Wear Daily* on the morning of the Gala. 'I dreamt of Joan of Arc one night and called Versace and was like, "What if we did something to reference Joan of Arc?" They came back with really, really great sketches.'

Having been appointed global ambassador for the Tommy Hilfiger womenswear division in October 2018, March 2019 saw Zendaya unveiling her debut fashion collaboration with the US designer. It had been a no-brainer for Hilfiger to sign her with his label, pointing out that her commitment to social justice was key to her appeal. 'There are so many celebrities with big social-media followings,' Hilfiger told *Vogue*, 'but are they going to make a difference in society? Right from our first conversations, it was clear she intends to use her celebrity to fight for change. She's got the heart of an activist.'

The collection was launched in Paris and boasted a star-studded line-up of fifty-nine Black models, aged from eighteen to seventy, and finishing off with a powerhouse performance by Grace Jones. The collection was inspired by 1973's 'Battle of Versailles', the legendary fashion face-off that brought the likes of Grace Kelly and Andy Warhol together to see couturiers Pierre Cardin and Yves Saint Laurent compete against American upstarts Halston and Anne Klein. The evening put Black models and American fashion front and centre on the world stage.

'Without these women [...] opening those doors, we wouldn't be here,' said Zendaya, who had asked that original Versailles Black supermodel Pat Cleveland be included in the show, which featured multicoloured metallic dresses, white bell-bottoms and lots and lots of Lurex. 'So, it's about celebrating them.'

It was also an homage to the total fabulousness that had been 1970s fashion. In addition to the Versailles sartorial ding-dong, Zendaya and Law referenced *Charlie's Angels*, Sonny and Cher, singer Lola Falana and broadcaster Jayne Kennedy in the show – for which Hilfiger allowed them free rein.

'Tommy gave us the keys,' Law told *The Hollywood Reporter*. '"Whatever you want to do, just do it," from conception to hair and makeup and casting to the collection on the runway.'

Zendaya herself brought inspiration boards from the 1970s, including pictures from her family album. The result was, as Zendaya attested, 'bold and classic'. People were on their feet after the show – not a regular Paris Fashion Week occurrence by any means. Zendaya was overwhelmed to come backstage and be hugged by all these beautiful Black models who had unwittingly opened doors for artists like her.

'Our show was a celebration and appreciation for all of the iconic women who fearlessly pioneered and opened doors that are the very reason I'm able to exist in this space,' Zendaya wrote in an Instagram post. 'So, to every woman on that stage and the many others who weren't, we love you, we see you and we thank you.'

At the 2019 Met Gala, Zendaya pulled out all the stops yet again. The theme was 'Camp: Notes on Fashion' and while some attendees took this literally, Zendaya and Law's collaboration delivered not only a fashion statement but a spectacle, complete with an exaggerated narrative and performance. It was also, in part, homage to Zendaya's Disney past. She arrived at the Met dressed as Disney's iconic Cinderella in a custom-made gown by Tommy Hilfiger that featured a powder blue tulle overlay, a corseted bodice and exaggerated sleeves, as per the original, beloved ball gown from the 1950 feature-length animation. Zendaya wore a blonde wig in a simple updo, complete with blue headband, plus a simple black choker around her neck. Law was her Fairy Godmother who, with a few waves of his wand, expelled a magical mist and lit up Zendaya's gown, which began to twinkle in front of the cameras and slowly light up from the bottom (the lights were hidden within the fabric of the garment). When fully illuminated, it resembled a chic Christmas tree. Ever the perfectionist, Zendaya's purse was modelled in the shape of a tiny, bejewelled glass coach and as she glided off the pink carpet, one glass slipper was left abandoned.

'Zendaya loves drama,' Law revealed to *Women's Wear Daily*, 'When you have someone who thrives off it, who loves it, who's addicted to fashion, we can go drama.'

The fashion world regarded Zendaya's costume and the theatre surrounding it as the best, most enchanting moment of the evening. But not everyone was impressed. Her fellow Disney alumnus Lindsay Lohan took to Instagram to mock Zendaya's look, claiming actress Claire Danes had worn a similar outfit first in 2016. 'Claire Danes did that with Zac Posen already,' Lohan posted. Tagging Claire directly, she added, 'You wore this dress so beautifully, I don't know why someone thinks that they can be more chic. Ever.'

As ever, Zendaya's response was gracious, measured and philosophical. Speaking to the UK's *Daily Telegraph* she said, 'I didn't feel hurt by it and it didn't make me sad because I have no idea what that person is going through. Maybe in some strange way, that comment made them feel better that day. People are only negative because negativity is eating away at them.'

Meanwhile she had been courted and signed up by the prestige French cosmetics brand Lancôme to join its star-studded roster of beauty ambassadors, alongside the likes of Julia Roberts, Lupita Nyong'o and Kate Winslet.

'We look forward to a joyous future with Zendaya, whose charisma, influence in film, music and fashion is undoubted,' announced Françoise Lehmann, Lancôme's global brand president, in a statement. 'Zendaya brings a youthful and a unique approach to beauty that perfectly complements Lancôme's vision and creativity.'

Zendaya was equally complimentary in return: 'It's a huge honor to be able to represent a brand like Lancôme and join such an incredible line-up of iconic women,' she announced.

What was next for her? Zendaya had heard on the film industry grapevine about the remake of an epic 1984 sci-fi blockbuster that was currently in development and had been greenlit for production. In much the same way as she'd set her heart on the part of 'girl in movie' in *Spider-Man: Homecoming*, her sights were set on this project, too. She wanted in – and nothing was going to stop her.

All Made Up!

She may have been a Cover Girl muse for a while before luxury French brand Lancôme named her as a global ambassador in 2019, but Zendaya was a relatively late starter when it came to make-up. She was never one of those little girls who, aged five or so, was already raiding their mother's cosmetics bag and slapping on the slap. For a start, her mother, Claire, never wore make-up when 'lil Daya was growing up, and she wasn't raised believing that she had to wear it or do her hair in a certain way to feel beautiful. It was more about having fun. A natural beauty, Zendaya didn't start to really experiment with make-up until she started going to auditions in LA as a tween. Having landed the role of Rocky in *Shake It Up*, she began making red carpet appearances, and by the time she was thirteen she was rocking a lick of sparkly lip gloss, subtly applied mascara and wearing cute hair slides, or barrettes as they are known in the USA, in her hair. Within two years, she was also using blush, incorporating shimmery eyeshadow and experimenting with bold lip colours. She was becoming more

ABOVE / Shaking It Up!
Newly famous Zendaya
signs autographs for
her fans in Paris, May
2012.

**RIGHT / Ready to
Launch!** Promoting her
first book *Between U
and Me*, and first album
Zendaya, New York,
October 2014.

OPPOSITE / Venus in Vivienne Westwood: Attending the 87th Academy Awards in Hollywood, February 2015.

RIGHT / Fashionista Sista: With style guru and brother-from-another-mother Law Roach at the Dolce & Gabbana New Vision and Millennials Party in Los Angeles, March 2017.

BELOW / Family Ties: Zendaya with her parents Kazembe Coleman and Claire Stoermer at the Q012 Performance Theater in Pennsylvania, October 2013.

ABOVE / Spidey Fun!
Zendaya with Spider-Man co-star and future boyfriend Tom Holland at a publicity junket for *Spider-Man: Homecoming* in London, June 2017.

LEFT / Safe with Spidey: On set filming *Spider-Man: Far From Home* in New York, 2018.

Queen of the Met: Zendaya channels Joan of Arc as imagined by Versace for the Heavenly Bodies themed Met Gala in New York, May 2018.

ABOVE / Soul Mates: Zendaya as Rue with co-star Hunter Schafer as Jules in the first series of ground-breaking HBO drama, *Euphoria*, in 2019.

BELOW / Warrior Princess: With *Dune* co-star Timothée Chalamet at the London premiere of the movie in October 2021.

LEFT / Dune Swoon:
Walking and wowing the red carpet in wet-look leather Balmain at the premiere of *Dune* during the 78th Venice International Film Festival, September 2021.

RIGHT / Sexy Spider Girl!
Rocking the red carpet in Valentino for the LA premiere of *Spider-Man: No Way Home* in Los Angeles, December 2021.

ABOVE / Euphoric! Zendaya makes Emmys history by winning her second award for playing Rue in *Euphoria*, Los Angeles, September 2022.

LEFT / Pretty in Pink: Attending the Valentino Womenswear Fall/Winter 2022/2023 show at Paris Fashion Week, March 2022.

confident and daring about her hair styles, too – creatively experimenting with wigs and hair extensions to achieve the look she was going for, whether that be a blonde bob, cornrows, waist-length and ramrod straight, Afro, wavy old-school Hollywood glamour or locs.

As with all things Zendaya, she made up her own rules when it came to beauty. 'If you're asking for the answers, they don't exist,' she told Brydie website. 'Beauty has no definition, and if you do create a definition for yourself as you grow older, it's ever-changing. It'll be very different from when you're 18 years old to when you're 22 and 30. Take your time.'

She has said more than once that it's more fun to experiment rather than replicate the same look over and over. However, she does have some favourites. 'I'm a sucker for classic neutral tones, you know, just browns,' she revealed to *Vogue*. 'They're easier to blend, for one thing – you don't have to be so precise. If you make a mistake, you can just add some more, no big deal. All that said, I do love a yellow eyeshadow! Or a very yellow-gold. I also appreciate a plain red lip, with nothing else on the eye or just a little mascara. When you find the right red, that can change everything, you know? It's got to be bright enough, deep enough, not too blue, not too this, not too that. I usually just go for a simple matte red.'

She also loves shimmer powder and calls 'shimmery stuff' her secret weapon. After applying make-up, she'll apply shimmer powder and says it's astounding how peachy and glowy her complexion looks as a result.

As a teenager, Zendaya spent hours watching make-up tutorials on YouTube. Later on, having been made-up by countless make-up artists over the years, it was inevitable that Zendaya would pick up tips from the professionals. 'Once I started working with make-up artists, I'd just watch them. If I liked the way someone did my eyebrows, I'd just watch how they did it and try it at home,' she told *Vogue*. 'Over time, learning to do my make-up became about taking different techniques and products from people I liked and putting them into my Rolodex. Then it was a matter of trial and error. I'd go out on the red carpet and later look at photos. Sometimes, I'd be like, "Ooh, I look like a ghost," so then I'd fix it the next time around. It's really about trying, failing, and trying again.'

If she had time, Zendaya would, on occasion, do her own make-up for events – she still does at times. She finds the process very therapeutic, particularly if she's ever stressed out before a press junket, red carpet or big event. There is something about taking time to just be with herself that is relaxing for her.

When Zendaya's not working, attending a red carpet event, or out on the town with family and friends, she prefers to go barefaced. She likes looking natural, plus she feels it gives her skin a much-needed break. As for skincare, there are a few hard-and-fast rules she insists on sticking to: cleanser, toner, moisturizer. As with applying her own make-up, she enjoys the ritual. 'I never skip moisturizer,' she told *Vogue*. 'I feel like my face would just crack in half. Also, I do not sleep with make-up on. That's a big rule.'

Zendaya likes to incorporate different serums every now and then. She also likes to switch up her skincare so that her skin doesn't get too used to one brand, saying that her products always seem more effective when she's left them for a bit and then come back. When it comes to products she couldn't live without, concealer is first on her list. She also loves a brow product, whether it's a tinted brow gel or a brow pencil. She admits to being in love with her brows – but then aren't we all? 'How to get brows like Zendaya?' is one of the most asked beauty questions on the internet. She has let hers grow out and uses different brow products to alter their shape and density. By doing so, she is able to change her whole look.

Being a natural beauty but one who also uses make-up products in the most creative way possible, it was a natural choice when she became the face of Cover Girl cosmetics in 2016, before luxury brand Lancôme chose her as an ambassador in 2020.

As for Zendaya's hair? When she's not rocking a wig, she prefers to keep it au naturel. 'I like to wear my hair natural,' she told *Allure* magazine. 'My natural curl pattern came back after I stopped putting heat on my hair so I try to just embrace while learning to care for my natural hair. When I hit 15, [my hair] had been so fried [on sets] that it was falling out in the sink. Heat is the enemy. I find other ways to achieve the styles I want – pin-curling overnight, a roller set under a dryer with low, cool air. It takes more time, but it's worth it.'

Last but not least, Zendaya has loved rocking a nail-art manicure since her *Shake It Up* days. These days, she employs the services of graffiti-artist-turned-nail-artist Chaun Legend when she's in LA. However, she's happy to frequent nail salons used by us lesser mortals when she's away from home. But she is extremely picky about one thing: a chipped manicure. Her nails are either perfectly painted or left natural. Same goes for her beauty and make-up routine as a whole.

SIX

A Dune Deal

'I have become a *Dune* nerd, for sure
– I'm very, very excited. I feel so lucky,
incredibly lucky to be a part of it. It's
such a beautiful thing and I'm geeking
out like everyone else.' – **Zendaya**

on *The Late Show with Stephen Colbert*

Following a thwarted attempt in the 1970s, Frank Herbert's best-selling sci-fi epic *Dune* had finally made it to the big screen in 1984. A big-budget production with a mega-star line-up that included Patrick Stewart, Kyle MacLachlan and the singer Sting, the David Lynch written-and-directed blockbuster bombed at the box office and was pulled from movie theatres and cinemas within five weeks of its release, with Lynch largely disowning the production. Fast forward three decades and it was felt in Hollywood that a remake – or rather a new adaptation of Herbert's original first book – was long overdue. In November 2016, Legendary Entertainment acquired the rights to make a new Dune film with *Prisoners*, *Arrival* and *Bladerunner 2049* French-Canadian director Denis Villeneuve coming on board a month later. Having read the book in his youth, he had spoken of directing a film version as his 'dream project'. Zendaya's dream project was to play Chani, the love interest of the main protagonist, Paul Atreides. Chani is a member of the Fremen, the native people of the planet Arrakis. Paul doesn't know who she is when she appears in his visions. They meet after his family arrives on the harsh desert land of Arrakis, aka Dune, and she becomes his protector, his guide and ultimately his lover and wife. The evolving relationship between Paul and Chani – which has repercussions not just for their lives, but for the planet Arrakis itself and possibly the entire galaxy – is a crucial element of the story, even if Chani is slow at first to warm to the Atreides heir.

'Before they were even looking at people, I heard about it. And I was like, "I really want to get in the room,"' she told *Vogue*. 'They weren't looking in my direction. And I was like, "Hey, I'm here!"'

In preparation for the audition, Zendaya read Herbert's novel and was surprised but certainly not displeased to feel a real connection with the book shortly after she started it. The world of *Dune* felt eerily familiar to her, and she mentioned this to her mother, Claire, who informed her that her father, Zendaya's grandfather, had been a massive fan of the Dune stories and had displayed the volumes in his home. This really brough home to Zendaya just how important this mysterious, unreal world was to fans – it was somewhere they'd been able to escape to for years.

Zendaya had watched Villeneuve's thriller *Prisoners* over and over. She longed to work with him, especially on a film that had the potential to be absolutely epic and where she may have the opportunity to play a character from another planet. She suspected she wasn't on the film-makers' radar, but fearless as ever, she did what she has done before in similar situations: she persuaded the powers-that-be to see her in the hope they'd be blown away by her. As with the Spider-Man franchise, the strategy worked. Villeneuve saw a lot of actresses for the role, but on meeting Zendaya, she immediately made him believe that she had been raised on an alien planet, in the deep desert, in the roughest environment. He later said that he had been particularly amazed by the high precision of her acting skills, her intelligence, her graceful patience and her great generosity. She was, he proclaimed, one of the most professional artists he had ever worked with and revealed, in retrospect, that he regretted subjecting her to the audition process, but it was just because he hadn't known her then.

Zendaya later revealed to *W* magazine that her 'chemistry read' with Timothée Chalamet, who had been cast to play Paul Atreides, had been particularly nerve-racking. 'I had just gotten my wisdom teeth taken out,' she said. 'My biggest fear was that my mouth would be vile, and then I would have to do a scene with Timothée where we have to be really close, and he would smell my possible dry socket breath.'

She was, as it turned out, worrying unnecessarily. There was no dry socket breath. There was, however, a palpable chemistry between Zendaya and Timothée. Each recognized a kindred spirit in the other from the off. 'I became very close with Timothée,' she told *Entertainment Weekly*. 'We were like, "Oh, this is great, we're gonna be besties, I can tell."'

Chani's role in the first *Dune* film of the hoped-for franchise was small, but it promised great things for the second movie, which they hoped would be greenlit soon after the release – and success – of the first. Zendaya travelled to the Middle East in summer 2019 to shoot her scenes. The majority of the Arrakis scenes were filmed at Jordan's Wadi Rum, also known as the Valley of the Moon. It is a dry, massively raw, unforgiving landscape that feels like it goes on forever. Zendaya was utterly captivated. She had never been anywhere like it before – and what's more, this unique part of the world was where she would be working, even if only for a few days!

As with Sam Levinson on *Euphoria*, Villeneuve was her go-to reference on all things Chani. She discussed the role at length with Villeneuve, and for any question she had about her character, the detailed-oriented director had an answer. Zendaya described part of the process for developing her character to *Empire* magazine: 'Chani is a fighter – that's what her people are. I only really had a few days with her, so I kind of scratched the surface but it was so much fun figuring her out. What does she walk like, what does she talk like? This is her planet, so how does she navigate this world? It was so fun.'

Her time on-set was only a matter of days. Short though the shoot may have been, it was undeniably sweet for her and left an indelible impression. She felt she had learned so much as an actress and had become better just from the experience of being around Denis, watching him interact with his actors and run sets. 'He's so kind and attentive to all of his actors. I was only there for four days and I did not want to leave! Denis understands what he wants from us but he's also very collaborative, allowing me to have my take on the character as well. I don't want to jinx anything but I can't wait to explore her more. I hope I get to learn more from Denis. I love to learn from people who are great at their job.'

At the end of the week, she seriously hadn't wanted to leave. She had discovered that Denis had a sense of warmth that created a real feeling of family and community among the company. She felt immediately at home and very welcomed by the cast and crew who were, she said, simply lovely. It was an environment of mutual respect and support, overseen by a director with a strong, guiding vision and who was open to everyone's input. The close-knit nature of the cast, despite the massive scale of the production, led Timothée to describe the experience as 'an indie film on steroids'. On location, the bond between Zendaya and Timothée deepened. She discovered that not only was Timothée a very talented actor, but also a wonderful person and a good friend. She had found somebody who could absolutely relate to what her life was like and who she could talk to about it. He had, she said, like Law and Darnell before him, become like family to her.

'I was the only other person closer to his age on the cast. So, he was like, "Awesome, someone who understands my jokes!" We had so much fun, too,' she explained to *Empire* magazine. When not on-set, they threw dance parties in Zendaya's trailer. 'He just rolled up with his little boom box and 2000s dance songs like "Soulja Boy".' Their illustrious co-star Javier Bardem turned up on one occasion and Zendaya snapped a polaroid of him busting some moves.

She had been greatly looking forward to playing Chani, but the reality surpassed even her own expectations. She'd always been a huge fan of sci-fi films and had longed to be involved in a truly epic one. *Dune* was that alright, but it literally felt like being part of another world. 'Just being there was incredible,' she told Den of Geek. 'I was blown away by the entire space immediately, working with Denis and Timothée and everybody.' Timothée himself would later interview her for *Elle* magazine, and when he asked her how the *Dune* shoot had been for her, she replied, 'Oh, man. I had a great fricking time. I felt like such a badass, just wearing that suit and walking around on these beautiful rock formations. It felt cool and so exciting to be part of the magic.'

Just as magical for Villeneuve was Zendaya's performance as Chani. She may not have had a huge role in the film, but nevertheless Villeneuve found himself giving her the spotlight.

'As the movie was evolving, Chani just kept growing and growing because I just was fascinated by Zendaya and her presence and how magnetic she was,' he told winteriscoming.com. 'I shot more and more scenes with her. We improvised stuff. I was just so inspired by her.'

In addition to her Dune adventure that summer, Zendaya was also busy on the press tour for *Spider-Man: Far From Home*, which was released on 26 June. As with junkets for the previous Spidey film, the vibe between her and Tom Holland was very relaxed. They hung out with co-stars Jake Gyllenhaal and Jacob Batalon at Disneyland in Anaheim, California, and spent time in Holland's home city, London, graciously doing the PR and interview thing over and over again. Tom credited Zendaya with teaching him how to deal with fame.

'Having her in my life was so instrumental to my sanity,' he revealed to Yahoo Entertainment. 'She is so good at being the role model for young guys and girls. When anyone comes up, like, "Can I have a picture?", it's never a bad time. Whereas my initial reaction was: "Why are you talking to me? Leave me alone."'

Tom continued to heap praise on Zendaya throughout the press tour. He explained how he and Zendaya, along with co-star Jacob Batalon, had become best friends while shooting their first *Spider-Man* film, and also revealed how helpful Zendaya had been as his life started to change. Her advice had made him behave differently as a result. He knew she was right – he was now a role model to millions rather than an anonymous actor from the London suburbs.

Zendaya taught Tom that fame and being constantly recognized by fans was work, too. So, he learned to smile for every picture, hug every fan, do the meet and greets at

Disneyland. To always be 'on' when out and about, no matter how wearing this might be. In 2022, he related a story about while he was walking through London a few years earlier, when a group of guys had started following him and taking pictures. 'Something had happened in my life and it really put me in a bad mood,' he explained, again to Yahoo. 'I was just trying to keep my head together, and I turned around and told them to get lost.' But after a short distance, Holland turned around and apologized. 'I have to remind myself that being Spider-Man is more of a responsibility than just having a job,' he added. 'There are kids out there who are bullied at school who don't fit in, and Spider-Man is their go-to guy, you know? And at the moment I'm that guy.'

Tom had come to realize that having Zendaya as a friend was invaluable to the success and happiness of both his life and career. Zendaya, for her part, was pretty darned flattering about Tom. She spoke of admiring him for the way he handled the pressure of being Spider-Man and having to play the superhero at all times. She was in tune with his perfectionist traits, and loved that he was funny, charismatic, a good listener, great fun and very comfortable to be around.

With such a mutual admiration society, it was inevitable there would be speculation about the two being an item – as indeed there had been since they'd been cast in *Spider-Man: Homecoming.* There were even rumours of them holidaying together in Europe. Zendaya shut these down immediately. Of course they were together in Europe! They were doing press for the movie!

The looks she was putting out while on this press tour had fashion magazines, websites and her millions of fans and followers positively drooling. The gorgeous cobalt blue dress and killer pair of sparkly black-and-silver wrap-around heels she wore following her appearance on *The Late Show with Stephen Colbert*; the playful orange Carolina Herrera minidress and matching silk scarf with white Christian Louboutin heels she wore for the show itself; a pyjama-inspired head-to-toe red patterned Fendi ensemble she modelled during a visit to the MTV studios in New York City; a Dice Kayek monochrome leather coat she sported on another visit; satiny gunmetal grey Peter Do separates for the *Spider-Man: Far From Home* ceremonial lighting at the Empire State Building; another shiny Peter Do look in blue as she walked around the city; yet another Do design – a translucent midi dress over matching trousers, both featuring a car blueprint pattern – for an appearance on *Good Morning America* in New York. In London, her style was a tad more formal. For the cast dinner at Cartier Bond Street, she chose a wine-coloured Neil Barrett look with Giuseppe Zanotti heels. She dressed in striped separates from Emilio Pucci for the *Spider-Man: Far From Home* Facebook Live session and photocall at the Corinthia Hotel in London. Another inspired choice was the photocall at the Tower of London, where she rocked a cravat and Alexandre Vauthier fitted jacket.

However she saved the best until last and was nothing short of a style wonder-woman at the movie premiere at the TCL Chinese Theatre in Hollywood in late June 2019. There were gasps from the assembled crowd as she emerged on the red carpet in a backless red-and-black sequined Armani Privé gown and Christian Louboutin heels. 'If she was Spider-Man,' quipped Law Roach on Instagram, 'this would be her suit.' For the after-party, Zendaya changed into an olive green, tiered, high-neck Balmain gown with perfectly placed cut-outs.

Spider-Man: Far From Home was released worldwide on 2 July 2019. In the main, the film received positive reviews with praise for its humour, action sequences, visuals, and the performances of Holland and Gyllenhaal. Zendaya was also praised: 'Zendaya shines, dropping razor-wire zingers with deadpan delight,' was the verdict of *Empire*. And Den of Geek noted that, 'Zendaya has an easy chemistry with Holland that is much more laid back than the romantic melodrama of the Tobey Maguire or Andrew Garfield eras.'

The film would go on to gross over $1.1 billion worldwide, making it the first Spidey film to pass the billion-dollar mark. It was the fourth-highest-grossing film of 2019 and became Sony Pictures' highest-grossing film.

Once her *Spider-Man* duties were done and dusted, and on hearing the very welcome news that *Euphoria* was on track for a second season, Zendaya decided to go decidedly left field (for her) and take a holiday – the first proper holiday she'd enjoyed in all her years! She took a trip to Greece in August 2019, celebrating her twenty-third birthday there on 1 September. When she was spotted at the Acropolis in Athens with her *Euphoria* co-star Jacob Elordi – and especially once paparazzi had snapped him giving her a kiss – the rumour mill went into overdrive and sent her fans into a frenzy. Rue and Jules were an item! But even if they were, this was hardly a romantic trip for two: Law Roach and Darnell were both on the holiday, too – in fact, she allegedly handed Darnell her credit card so she wouldn't know how much she'd spent and therefore not get stressed about it. Members of her family were also present. 'I went on vacation with my family, which was very sweet,' she posted on Instagram. 'It was kind of just my first time just chilling, you know, I haven't chilled in a really long time. I, for the first time, kind of detached from the world for a little bit.' She also added that she was so removed that she was surprised to see her face on the Lancôme campaign when she got to the airport to return to LA.

Once back in the USA, Zendaya unveiled her second fashion collection for Tommy Hilfiger at the TOMMYNOW experiential runway event held at Harlem's iconic Apollo Theater during New York Fashion Week on 8 September 2019, with many of her *Euphoria* co-stars present to lend moral support. This TommyXZendaya Holiday 2019 collection was described as a celebration of era-defining 1970s and 80s power dressing redefined with a bold and modern edge. Highlights included a striped, metallic knit maxi dress; a constellation print, metallic, silk-blend dress and blouse; and a black velvet, single-button blazer and tuxedo pants.

'Signature houndstooth and polka dot prints in unexpected proportions bring a unique play to maxi skirts and wrap dresses,' read the publicity material. 'Warm burgundy hues mix with metallics and monochrome palettes for a fresh edge. Luxurious fabrics bring the collection together, from creamy leathers and faux furs, to rich velvets and premium denim. With powerful, inspirational women at its heart, timeless silhouettes are reinvented for a new era.'

In late September, Zendaya was a presenter at the 71st Emmy Awards, bringing her usual red carpet magic to the proceedings. With her hair loose and flowing, she wore a custom Vera Wang emerald green sheer corset dress with a high leg slit, matching pumps and accessorizing Cartier jewellery. *Harper's Bazaar* dubbed her a 'Green Goddess'. Six weeks later she was accepting not one but two awards of her own. At the People's Choice Awards, she won Best Drama TV Star for *Euphoria* and Best Female Movie Star for *Spider-Man: Far From Home*. Wearing a cut-out black dress and Louboutin heels, she thanked the fans who had made *Euphoria* such an incredible success.

'*Euphoria* and Rue, I think, is one of the most beautiful things that's ever happened for me,' she said in her acceptance speech. 'Thank you to all of you for receiving it with open hearts. And to anyone who has felt seen by our show, on behalf of the cast and crew and everyone, that's all we really ever wanted. So thank you for allowing us to do that.'

At the tail end of the year – which had been an absolute vintage one for her – Zendaya travelled to Sydney, Australia, to collect her *GQ Australia* Woman of the Year award. She couldn't have looked more worthy of the award. Wearing her long hair loose and sporting natural-looking make-up, she wore a white suit jacket that hit just above the waist and a coordinating long white skirt by Monot, Vhernier accessories and Christian Louboutin shoes.

'I don't think anyone has had a bigger year than Zendaya,' said *GQ* editor Mike Christensen ahead of the star's arrival. 'There has been a coming of age with her. She starred in *Spider-Man: Far From Home* and has also been the star of the show *Euphoria*. This year is her year, so it is amazing to have someone like her as our Woman of the Year. She is not just an actress; she is keen to make sure she has a huge following and that she is a role model to the younger generations.'

Taking to the podium to collect her award, Zendaya was as gracious and charming as she'd ever been. 'Thank you so much – this is an incredible honour,' she said. '"Woman of the Year" – that's kinda crazy as I'm twenty-three years old and I'm just figuring out how to be a young woman myself. Figuring it out as I go. I don't know what to say … it's a huge honour. Sometimes I just go and I go and I go and I just forget to stop and take in moments like this. Sometimes I think I work so much I forget about life. To actually be present in those kind of moments where you can actually look and take it all in for a second. Holy sh*t, this is happening! Pretty cool. Thank you for allowing me to use my art form to connect with people and to hopefully make a positive impact on their lives.'

As the twenty teens became the twenty twenties, Zendaya had so much to look forward to. Making another season of *Euphoria*, the anticipated release of *Dune*, the prospect of another Spidey film on the horizon. Her love life seemed to be thriving, too. Zendaya and Jacob were papped kissing in New York City. A source told E! Online in early 2020 that the two had been an item for over six months.

'Jacob and Zendaya have been seeing each other for months now,' the source said. 'They started as close friends but it became romantic after their show wrapped. They have been inseparable since last summer and have been making time for each other in between projects. Jacob has met Zendaya's family, and everyone adores him. They have a lot of fun together and have a lot in common.'

She attended the Critics' Choice Awards in January 2020, having been nominated for Best Actress in a Drama Series Category for playing Rue in *Euphoria*. She was up against tough competition: Christine Baranski (*The Good Fight*), Olivia Colman (*The Crown*), Jodie Comer (*Killing Eve*), Nicole Kidman (*Big Little Lies*), Regina King (*Watchmen*), Michaela Jaé (MJ) Rodriguez (*Pose*), and Sarah Snook (*Succession*). She lost out to Regina King but was the runaway winner in the fashion stakes, wearing a fuchsia, body-moulded Tom Ford breastplate with matching flowing skirt for the ceremony. She accessorized with Mateo New York earrings, Djula rings and Christian Louboutin heels.

Speaking to press on the red carpet, Zendaya revealed how *Euphoria* had taught her a lot about herself and had made her more confident in her own abilities, because she doubted herself a lot. It had pushed her and allowed her to fully explore her creativity. Before the show, she admitted, she hadn't had any work that pushed her to such an extent or allowed her to be so creative.

'I was looking for something to prove I can do it,' she continued. '*Euphoria* served as that, in the healthiest way. I never want to plateau as an actress – I always want to be able to explore and push myself. Being an actress brings me to places and makes me do things I'd probably never do.'

She had been due to start filming season two in March 2020 but then ... the world shut down!

Giving Back

Some stars are all take, take, take. Not Zendaya. Right from her earliest days as a Disney kid, she's been highly appreciative of her good fortune and determined to give something back.

In December 2011, she donated a percentage of the budget for her 'Swag It Out' video to support the 'Toys for Tots' effort that, every Christmas, gave thousands of gifts to underprivileged children. She also, along with several other Disney stars, served as a 'Friend for Change' ambassador, helping kids make changes that would positively affect other people, local communities and the planet. Zendaya and her *Shake It Up* co-star Bella Thorne led the charge to encourage kids everywhere to volunteer to become leaders. She and Bella also teamed up with *Seventeen* magazine and the organization 'Donate My Dress' to spread the word about enabling underprivileged girls to attend their high school prom. Zendaya publicized the event and donated her own dress for the cause. On both her fifteenth and sixteenth birthdays, Zendaya donated book bags to local elementary schools in her hometown of Oakland.

In October 2012, Zendaya performed at the Los Angeles

Sports Arena. The show benefited Operation Smile, an organization that helps treat children born with cleft lips and cleft palates. Also, that October, Zendaya announced that she had teamed up with the Convoy of Hope charity to raise $1,000,000 to help victims of Storm Sandy, which had devastated the East Coast of the USA. She went on to promote other relief efforts for the organization and, in 2014, Zendaya, along with singer MAX and singer/songwriter and music producer Kurt Schneider, recorded a cover of John Legend's 'All of Me' with a percentage of the proceeds donated to Operation Smile. She fronted UNICEF's Trick-or-Treat campaign that same year before travelling to South Africa in July 2015 on behalf of UNAIDS, the United Nations' charity programme set up to help prevent HIV and AIDS while also providing access to treatments. In addition, she was involved in another fundraiser for CrowdRise, with proceeds going to another AIDS-linked charity in Soweto.

Most millennials spend their birthdays wildly celebrating and partying with friends. Not Zendaya. While she enjoyed low-key celebrations with family, she consistently donated to charity for her eighteenth, nineteenth and twentieth birthdays. Her first altruistic birthday effort, on her eighteenth birthday, was to host an event raising funds to feed more than 100 malnourished children in Haiti, Tanzania and the Philippines. This was in alliance with the organization feedONE, an initiative of the Convoy of Hope, which aids those who lack resources for food around the world.

'Too many kids will go back to school hungry this year, but we can do something about that,' Zendaya said to the Convoy of Hope. 'My generation has the opportunity to change the world. With Convoy of Hope, I've raised my voice and am using it to give people hope.'

For her nineteenth birthday, following another trip to South Africa, where she had met three brothers whose parents had died of AIDS and who, as a result, were living in appalling conditions, Zendaya hosted a fundraiser with the UNAIDS Foundation. For her twentieth birthday, she again joined forces with Convoy of Hope to host a campaign and raise $50,000 in support of its Women's Empowerment Initiative. 'I want to help raise money for women who are impoverished,' Zendaya said to her supporters. 'This program helps them take care of themselves and their families, breaking the cycle of poverty.' The fundraiser aided women living in El Salvador, Tanzania, Kenya, the Philippines and Nicaragua.

'We are so grateful for Zendaya's heart to help women in need,' said Hal Donaldson, co-founder and president of Convoy of Hope. 'She is enabling us to bring strength and dignity to people throughout the world.'

In September 2017, she partnered with Verizon Foundation as a spokesperson for their national #weneedmore initiative to bring technology, access and learning opportunities to children. She was also empowering them to pursue careers in STEM (science, technology, engineering and mathematics). In March 2018, Zendaya teamed up with Google.org and its 'bring the best of Google' mission to give back to students at a community school in Oakland, funding an innovative computer science curriculum. As a person with a lifelong abhorrence of bullying, in October 2013, she took part in Proctor and Gamble's anti-bullying campaign 'Mean Stinks' and co-hosted the nationwide live-streamed assembly joined by almost 500 schools. In September 2017, along with her *Spider-Man: Homecoming* co-stars, she fronted a public service announcement awareness campaign, STOMP Out Bullying. Then two years later, in partnership with Yoobi, a charity donating supplies to schools, she surprised students at the Global Family Elementary School in her native Oakland.

'Thank you @yoobi for helping me surprise every student at a very special school in my hometown of Oakland with school supplies to start the school year off right!' was Zendaya's caption in a sweet Instagram story selfie of herself with a group of the kids.

The day was documented on the charity's Instagram page. 'Hey, it's Zendaya here,' she said in a video. 'I'm in my hometown in Oakland and we are at an amazing school and we're about to surprise all the kids with school supplies. They're in there, they don't know I'm here yet!'

Zendaya has always been a feminist. As early as 2015 she explained to *Flare* magazine her definition of the term: 'A feminist is a person who believes in the power of women just as much as they believe in the power of anyone else. It's equality, it's fairness and I think it's a great thing to be part of.'

After attending a women's march to show her support for women's rights in Washington, D.C., in January 2017, she stated in *Vogue* magazine that feminism should encompass, 'Women who look like you, women who don't look like you, women whose experiences are different than you.'

On many occasions Zendaya has talked about her experiences as a Black female actor in Hollywood, and she has made good use of her social media platforms to highlight issues referring to racial injustice in addition to those involving body shaming and bullying. She is a supporter of the Black Lives Matter movement, took part in the George Floyd protests in 2020 and temporarily put her Instagram account at the disposal of Patrisse Cullors, co-founder of BLM, in order to spread awareness and share anti-racism resources. Zendaya has continued to call out racism and vigorously advocate for Black women and the struggles they face. She has said that if she were to direct or create a film, she would hire Black actresses for lead roles. A fierce advocate for the arts, Zendaya believes artistic projects can bring about change. After 'Loc-gate' at the 2015 Oscars, Zendaya, at just eighteen years old, proved that everyone has a voice. She voiced her beliefs and values in a dignified and rational manner, and in doing so won the support of many, while she also advocated for change that would benefit humanity. On the back of what happened, Zendaya was presented with a 'Young Luminary Award' at Pennsylvania State University. In her acceptance speech, she announced, 'There's so much inspiration here in this room. There's no age limit to being able to help people and just being able to inspire others and I just want to be living proof of that.'

Since the 2015 Oscars, Zendaya has consistently continued to use her celebrity to meaningfully talk about race and social justice.

'I am inspired right now by people who *use* their platforms,' she explained in a 2017 interview with *Glamour* magazine. 'If people know your name, they should know it for a reason.'

She often talks about how she feels she has a responsibility to help represent the Black community on-screen. She has spoken of her own struggles to get inside an audition room for parts that are intended for white actresses, and she is tireless in her fight for diversity in Hollywood. In 2018, she revealed to *Marie Claire*, 'I always tell my theatrical manager, "Anytime it says they're looking for white girls, send me out. Let me get in the room. Maybe they'll change their minds."'

She voices concerns about the ways in which her light skin makes it easier to land roles than her darker-skinned peers. 'I am Hollywood's, I guess you could say, acceptable version of a Black girl, and that needs to change,' she said at BeautyCon in 2018. 'We're vastly too beautiful and too interesting for me to be the only representation of that.'

She further elaborated on this theme to *The Hollywood Reporter* in 2020: 'I think it's important being a light-skinned woman to recognize my privilege in that sense as well and to make sure that I'm not taking up space where I don't need to.'

Zendaya is not only passionate about opening doors but also leaving them ajar for those artists who will come after her. Just like Halle Berry, Angela Bassett and Beyoncé did for her.

Over the years Zendaya has been a keen advocate for voting. In October 2016, she was one of the celebrities to participate in the 'Vote Your Future' initiative and appeared in a campaign video. In September 2020, along with former First Lady Michelle Obama, she encouraged young women to check their voter registration ahead of elections. The next month, she shared a video while casting her vote to re-remind people to vote. Zendaya's advocacy on behalf of the LGBTQ+ community is well-known and she has received praise from the transgender community for highlighting the cause on *Euphoria,* where her character, Rue, is romantically involved with a trans girl, Jules, who is played by the transgender actress and model Hunter Shafer.

Zendaya is a perfect role-model for the young women of the world. She not only fights for all women but makes it her life's mission to champion women in all their complexities. She has always been unique in Hollywood, from her down-to-earth personality to her unapologetic honesty. While not the only actor to fight for women's rights and countless other causes, Zendaya deserves similar recognition to stars such as the much-feted Angelina Jolie. She sees the injustices of the world and does everything in her power to change the status quo. We should all strive to be more Zendaya.

SEVEN

Locked Down

'I don't really know Zendaya outside
of the Zendaya who works.' – **Zendaya
talking to *Entertainment Tonight* via
Zoom during the Covid-19 pandemic**

Zendaya didn't know what to do with herself. For over ten years – apart from that one holiday to Greece – she'd never stopped working. Working as hard as it was possible to work with practically every hour of every day accounted for. She could be filming, going to meetings for exciting new projects, travelling the world to shoot on location or to publicize her latest movie or TV project, or doing in-person interviews, high fashion magazine shoots, red carpet events or awards ceremonies.

She spent the earliest days of the pandemic working on the second series of *Euphoria*. She'd been all geared up for it. But in March 2020, just days after the first cast reading of the script, Hollywood safety protocols shut down productions across the city – and now? Nothing. Nada. Zilch. Not now the curse of Covid-19 was worming its sinister way around the globe and curtailing her – and everyone else's – life. She knew she shouldn't complain. And she didn't complain, except only to herself within the confines of her own mind. Across the world, hundreds of thousands were dying from this mysterious disease, while others were suffering from post-infection complications from which they might never fully recover. Countless more were mourning the loss of loved ones. There were also those who had seen their livelihoods crash and burn as a result of the pandemic. Zendaya was well aware how lucky she was. She was healthy, there was a job waiting for her once it was over, she had no money worries and she was isolating in the beautiful, spacious Californian ranch-style home that she had just bought in the sought-after Encino neighbourhood of Los Angeles. The new place, originally built in 1939, was said to be stunning. Measuring 5,000 square feet (465 m²) and sat on 4 acres (1.6 ha), it boasted six bedrooms, seven bathrooms, a two-bedroom guest house, a stunning pool and several other luxury amenities. For the most part, the sun was constantly shining, too. But still, she had worked consistently since she was just thirteen years old. So, when she suddenly had nothing but free time, she was questioning herself, 'What do I do with this? Who am I without my job? How do I find purpose and meaning?' She didn't even have any hobbies. Her hobby was what she did for a living. What she didn't do was free time. She liked being on-set – that was her social life. Time off bored her. She had once proclaimed in an interview with *Vogue,* 'I hate spare time – I just don't know what I'm doing when I'm not working.'

Stuck at home, Zendaya had to come to terms with the fact that she had a big adjustment in front of her. She had no choice but to sit tight. She spent lockdown isolating with her assistant, Darnell, and her dog, Noon. On occasional days off before the pandemic she would just hang at home and watch and rewatch her favourite Harry Potter movies – she identified as Gryffindor, it goes without saying – but obviously she couldn't do that day after day with no end in sight. Initially, she spent hours rearranging her wardrobes and organizing her make-up, including colour-coding her Lancôme lipsticks. She also binged a lot of television shows, often completing a season in a day. Trying to stay in a happy place, she watched quite a few animated films, such as her all-time favourite *Shrek*, as well as funny YouTube compilations of people falling over or dogs and cats doing kooky things. But then what? Like so many of us during that strange time, she tried taking up new interests, such as painting – her *Euphoria* co-star Hunter Schafer had gifted her some oil paints.

'I think I'm pretty good,' she told *InStyle* magazine. 'I painted a female figure, and it was one of my first times trying oil paint. Hunter, who is one of the most special people in my life, is a phenomenal artist. Every now and then I'll whip out my kit and do a little something. She also inspired me to keep a sketchbook.'

The problem was, ever the perfectionist, Zendaya lost interest if she didn't feel she was producing artwork of a sufficiently superior standard, even though she'd never painted in her life before. If she wasn't immediately a Picasso, forget it! She bought a piano with the intention of learning how to play it over lockdown. She taught herself a three-chord tune which she dismissed as 'not very exciting'.

She needed something to keep her motivated. She told her assistant Darnell that she wanted to do more exercise, feeling it would help her mentally as well as physically, though it had never exactly been a favourite pastime.

'I tried in quarantine,' she later told *GQ* magazine. 'I did, like, maybe five days consistently ... I was like, "Yo, you know what, this is going to be my thing. I'm gonna keep my body active. I've got to do this." It didn't last very long.'

Then inspiration struck. Briefly. Zendaya decided to take advantage of the many wigs in her possession – courtesy of her countless appearances on red carpets over the years. Craving acting and missing her craft, she would pull on different wigs and pretend to be different characters, putting on a daily show for Darnell, which he would sometimes film on his phone. But this only took up an hour or so a day and it wasn't long before she tired of that, too. Likewise, doing the number puzzle Sudoku. Likewise, doing 'mindful' colouring. As lockdown continued, Zendaya found herself experiencing a personal crisis due to not being able to work.

'It was my first time just being like, "OK, who am I without this?"' she later told *People* magazine. 'Which is a very scary thing to confront and work through, because I don't really know Zendaya outside of the Zendaya who works. I didn't realize how much my job and my art were a part of my identity as a human.'

She would phone her mother in the middle of the night for reassurance. She found talking things out helped. At times she'd want Claire to stay on the line until she was asleep – 'like a frickin' baby,' she told *InStyle* magazine. She was, she realized, depressed. She was waking up every morning feeling bad and was continuing to feel bad all day. It felt like a dark cloud was hanging over her that she just couldn't get rid of. Some days, she would sleep until the afternoon, and occasionally she wouldn't get out of bed at all.

'It's like, "Well, what happened today?" "Well, I woke up, and that's it. I've pretty much been in bed all day,"' she recalled to *InStyle* magazine.

Therapy and talking things out helped set her on a more even keel, but she needed more. She needed a creative outlet. She needed to work! But how, when the whole of Hollywood was as good as closed? A kernel of a possible plan began to form. But realistically, was it doable? Sam Levinson, the creator of *Euphoria*, was who she turned to. Sam was like family and Zendaya spoke to him practically every day – and sometimes at night, too. Besides, she needed his input.

'I was in such a weird place. I was already struggling with "Who is Zendaya without her work?" I get everything from acting. It's my social life. It's my hobby. It's my fun thing to do. It's my challenge.' Zendaya later revealed to *The Hollywood*

Reporter. 'I asked Sam if there was a world in which we could shoot something in my house or somewhere else. There was no intention other than to allow us to all be creative together, and to get our crew from *Euphoria* paid.'

Levinson and Zendaya brainstormed ideas. A psychological horror film set in Zendaya's LA home was considered at one point, as was a one-character drama. Zendaya was fascinated with the idea of shooting a film with just two characters like a two-hander play – perhaps about a couple and their relationship. Then, a light bulb moment! A breakthrough! Sam thought back to an incident that had occurred between him and his wife a few years earlier. Back in September 2018, he had been mortified when he'd forgotten to thank his wife, Ashley Levinson, at the LA premiere of his film *Assassination Nation* – especially as Ashley happened to be a producer on the film in addition to being his wife. He had humbly apologized once back in his seat, but she smiled, told him not to worry and took his hand. This scenario inspired him and would, he decided, be the starting point of his lockdown movie. In the film, fictional writer-director Malcolm Elliot and his girlfriend Marie Jones return home from the premiere of his latest film where Malcolm, as Sam had done, neglected to thank his partner. But whereas in real life Ashley Levinson was magnanimous and forgiving, in the film, Marie is most definitely not. The incident opens up all kinds of tensions, jealousies and issues of resentment within their relationship – and beyond. Would Malcolm and Marie be able to find a way through or would it be game over?

Sam completed ten pages of the script on his first day of

writing. He called Zendaya and read them to her. She loved them, couldn't wait to play Marie and was excited about playing an adult woman for the first time in her life. She'd always played teenager roles on television and in film – and was still doing so. It was how people saw her, but this would be a real step forward, an evolution for her. It was still up in the air who would play Malcolm but Levinson had someone in mind: *BlacKkKlansman* actor John David Washington, who also had science fiction action-thriller film *Tenet,* directed by celebrated British/American filmmaker Christopher Nolan, in the can waiting for release. Managing to pull a few strings and get hold of his personal number, Sam cold-called John David, read out what he'd written and asked if he'd be interested in the project. It was an immediate yes.

'Everything had come to a halt and I was so desperate to work,' Washington told *The Hollywood Reporter*. 'Even with just those 10 pages, I knew I had to be part of it. It was something I desperately needed artistically. It was a godsend.'

In addition to acting in the production, Zendaya and Washington both invested their own money and became producers – as indeed did Sam Levinson, Ashley Levinson and several others involved in the production. The idea was that the entire crew would split any profits once the film was sold.

In June 2020, the cast and crew of the now-titled *Malcolm & Marie* decamped to the 500-acre (200 ha) Carmel Valley Ranch near the picturesque township of Carmel, situated just off the Pacific Highway south of San Francisco. Carmel was chosen because it was the only area in California where no permit was required to film on private property. A suitable house was sourced in which to film the movie, but before the shoot could get underway the cast and crew were required to quarantine for fourteen days at the luxury ranch resort, which was otherwise closed to guests. Covid testing took place at regular intervals.

'We abided by the strictest of protocols so that we could share them with our community. It was so important to us to help, if we could, to share a path forward, because so many people we cared about faced a disruption in income,' Ashley Levinson, Sam's producer wife, told *The Hollywood Reporter*.

The quarantine period also enabled Levinson, Zendaya, Washington and *Euphoria* cinematographer Marcell Rév to workshop and rehearse the script – although the last third of the screenplay wasn't completed until Levinson produced the final thirty pages the night before filming was due to commence. The film would be shot in black and white. While this was for aesthetic reasons, it was also because Zendaya felt it was important to reclaim the narrative of monochrome Hollywood where Black actors are concerned. The classic black and white Hollywood movies had only depicted Black characters as servants or slaves. Levinson was in full agreement.

'It felt like an interesting way to reclaim the glamour and iconography of that time and frame it in a different light,' he told *Backstage* magazine. 'Additionally, black-and-white immediately helps separate the audience from reality, allowing them to concentrate on the movie's subject matter rather than reality.'

Once the shoot started, strict Covid-19 protocols meant that the production and art teams had to work completely separately from the cast and crew. The former would work during the day, the latter from 9 p.m. to 5 a.m. Zendaya was wholly invested in the project. While all kinds of limits were in place due the pandemic – everyone was doing four jobs at once and there was no script supervisor or assistant director – what they had was also, in essence, limitless. There was no studio or stakeholder to answer to. It was totally their baby. This was a little nerve-racking and a big responsibility, but Zendaya relished the experience and was learning so much. There were also personal practicalities for her to consider. She was, for example, using her own clothes on-set and doing her own hair and make-up. There were times when she felt a little insecure, but these were fleeting. She felt grateful to be working and in awe of what they were able to achieve in such restricted circumstances and in such a short time. And she adored acting opposite Washington; she thought he was a brilliant actor and a great person, too. Zendaya felt proud of herself and this new chapter that had opened up in her life. She'd actually managed to 'up' her creativity at this very challenging time and learned to take the leap while doing so safely in quarantine. It had been a fascinating learning curve.

It was while Zendaya was involved with *Malcolm & Marie* that she received the news that she was to be invited to become a member of the Academy's Oscar voting committee. Historically, the committee had been made up almost exclusively of white men. According to a 2014 survey conducted by the *Los Angeles Times*, Oscar voters were on average sixty-three years old, 76 per cent of them were men and 94 per cent of them were white. After 2016's outcry around the significant lack of diversity, the Academy announced plans to address this, promising to double the number of women and ethnically diverse members by 2020. Thus, the Academy – or the Academy of Motion Picture Arts and Sciences (AMPAS) to give it its full name – invited 395 new members, of which 46 per cent were women and 39 per cent were people of colour. Zendaya was now one of them. To have influence at the Oscars? That was a very big deal. Little by little she was breaking down more barriers – even within this unprecedented time of pandemic.

After making *Malcolm & Marie*, Zendaya felt more like her old self. She felt creatively fulfilled. The work had enabled her to rediscover a personal joy that was like oxygen to her. She knew who she was when working – she was sure of herself and where she was heading. What was also joyous was the news, a few months after production had wrapped, that Netflix had purchased the worldwide rights to *Malcolm & Marie* to stream globally from early 2021 onwards. With little else to do, the world was watching more television than ever, so *Malcolm & Marie* would be seen by millions of viewers. What's more, both cast and crew would be rewarded handsomely, as $30 million dollars changed hands between the steaming service and the film-makers. Feeding America, a non-profit nationwide network of more than 200 food banks that fed more than 46 million people through food pantries, soup kitchens, shelters and other community-based agencies, also benefitted. In typical Zendaya fashion, she had factored in a percentage of the profits to go to the organization.

Although she undoubtedly felt happier in herself once the film had wrapped, Zendaya missed travelling and being free to do what she wanted. She got more good news: it was confirmed that her third Spider-Man film, *Spider-Man: No Way Home,* would start shooting towards the end of the year. It was later than originally planned, true, but there was a pandemic – so, all things considered, it was lucky it was happening at all. Nevertheless, she sensed a real despondency in the air due to a combination of Covid fatigue and the brutal murder of George Floyd by a police officer in Minneapolis. It was reported that Zendaya, along with several other Hollywood A-listers, was spotted at one of the Black Lives Matter (BLM) protests in Los Angeles. She revealed to co-founder of the BLM movement, Patrisse Cullors, in an interview with *InStyle* magazine, that Floyd's death had left her feeling helpless and devastated as well as deeply saddened. She didn't like to describe herself as a BLM activist, feeling that was a lifestyle, a choice a person made every day, to do the work and devote their life to the cause, and she didn't feel deserving of the title. There were many other words that better described what she did. She was an actress, but also just a person with a heart who wanted to do the right thing. She cared about people. She recalled being with her dad in Atlanta and filming the first *Spider-Man* film around the time that Philando Castile and Alton Sterling were killed by police. She'd been extremely emotional and concerned about Kazembe, who had been out for ages, supposedly picking up food. She'd called him and told him to come back to base immediately.

She didn't want him to go out and do anything. She'd been scared for his safety.

Zendaya went on to reveal to Cullors that she'd felt helpless in the wake of George Floyd's murder. 'I didn't know what I could do to help. And that's when I reach out to people like you. Because at the end of the day, I'm just an actress, you know? And I don't pretend to be anything other than that. If I don't know something, then I ask people who are actually on the front lines doing the work. I'm up in the bleachers, not on the field. So, I always think, "How can I cheer you on and be a part of something greater than myself?"'

Zendaya went on to tell her *Dune* co-star Timothée Chalamet, in an interview with *Elle* magazine, that it felt like the USA was going through a dark night of the soul, with her peers feeling hopeless, enraged, exhausted, and tired of living and growing up in a system that didn't feel like it was made for them. It was hard to find joy and beauty in life when life was so hard. Black people needed to embrace joy and not let it be taken away.

However, Zendaya added that witnessing her friends and peers speak out about America's complicated history with systemic racism and injustice also renewed her hope that things would get better. 'I find hope in my peers, the people who are out there on the streets doing the work – people I admire and I go to for advice and information on what's happening, so that I can make sure I'm using my platform in the most strategic way I can to help.'

Zendaya felt it was essential to not give up hope and faith in humanity. She knew many young people felt that the system had never worked for them, so why, in their case, should they even bother? But if anything positive could come out of this time, she felt that – along with despair – there was also some hope present. Changes were happening and she was inspired by her peers and their commitment. Those younger than her were, too. Zendaya's fifteen-year-old niece was about to go to high school, and she was deeply impressed to read her niece's Instagram posts and to listen to her thoughts about life, the hopes and dreams she had, and her quite clear understanding of things and how the world could be changed. Zendaya found this to be truly inspiring. Clearly there was still a sense of hope in young people of colour. This made 'Auntie Daya' want to keep going, to use her platform to tell people that their voices did matter and that they should continue to vocalize.

Zendaya made no comment about the fact that her supposed boyfriend, Jacob Elordi, was pictured enjoying dinner with model Kaia Gerber, his new girlfriend, on 1 September 2020 – Zendaya's twenty-fourth birthday. Whether there had never actually been in a proper relationship or there had been but it had just fizzled out, it didn't seem to be of much importance to her. She had other things on her mind; another dream was coming true. She had been nominated for an Emmy for Outstanding Lead Actress in a Drama Series for her role as Rue in *Euphoria.* But it would be the most low-key Emmys ever – a virtual event, due to the pandemic. There would be no red carpet, no glittering ceremony or Hollywood razzamatazz, but Zendaya was still determined to dress up for it.

'I definitely want to pull a look and maybe just walk my

living room carpet,' she revealed on the television show *Jimmy Kimmel Live!* shortly before the Emmys took place. 'I want to dress up. I still want to have the experience. It's different for sure, but I'm grateful either way.' She added that she would most likely spend the evening with her family and close friends at home in Los Angeles and treat her living room as a stand-in red carpet.

In the event, Zendaya got to dress up for the Emmys twice – because she wore two different gowns. She started the evening's proceedings in a stunning black and purple dress by Christopher John Rogers that featured a plunging neckline, puffy sleeves and a voluminous skirt that tapered in at the ankle. She also wore a pair of Christian Louboutin heels and sparkled in Bulgari jewels. She performed a little twirl for Law Roach's Instagram before changing into a second show-stopping look – a custom Giorgio Armani Privé gown. Styled with more Bulgari jewels, the polka-dot skirt and closely fitting, bikini-style sparkly top were just perfect – especially as it was while she was wearing this ensemble that she won her first Emmy, beating other big name nominees in her category, namely Jennifer Aniston, Olivia Colman and Sandra Oh. As Zendaya had predicted on *Jimmy Kimmel Live!*, she was in her sitting room surrounded by closest friends and family – her siblings, nephews, nieces, cousins and, of course, bursting-with-pride parents, Kazembe and Claire – when the announcement was made. As Zendaya was announced as the victor, the room erupted with screaming family members getting to their feet, punching the air and hugging each other. The girl herself looked ecstatic. Tears of happiness rolled down her cheeks and, surprised – she hardly ever cried in real life – she dabbed at them. The role of Rue had been by far the most challenging of career. She'd been so nervous that she wouldn't make a success of it. But she so, so had. What was more, she'd made history, too. She was the youngest artist in her category to ever winner an Emmy.

'This is pretty crazy!' Zendaya said in her acceptance speech. 'To the incredible cast and crew of *Euphoria* … I'm inspired by everything you do. To Sam Levinson, I appreciate you so much, you're my family.'

She also addressed the unreal circumstances of the past six months. 'This feels like a really weird time to be celebrating,' she continued. 'There is hope in the young people out there … to all my peers out there doing the work, I see you, I admire you … thank you.'

Zendaya later revealed to Timothée Chalamet in *Elle* magazine that standing outside each nominee's house on Emmys night had been a person in a hazmat suit, award in hand. If you won, the instructions were to grab it quickly from them before they exited. If you didn't, the hazmat person would promptly disappear into the night, taking the award away with them. In Zendaya's case, the award had actually been handed to Darnell, who then presented her with it.

'I was very nervous before the awards,' she added. 'I didn't want to write anything down because maybe it was bad luck to have anything prepared. But I did – just in case. That was helpful and I'm glad my family was there. Everybody was there, screaming, as my family does! We are a very loud family, and I was worried that they were going to be screaming for too long. And the little clock would start ticking, and I'd be like, "Ah, thank you." And then it would be over. It was so lovely to have them with me.'

A few weeks after her victory, and with the strictest Covid rules having been relaxed somewhat, Zendaya headed to Atlanta to start shooting *Spider-Man: No Way Home.* She was excited at the prospect of playing MJ again, and at the thought of being reunited with Jacob Batalon and Tom Holland – with Tom most of all.

Working It Out!

She has a body to die for, but Zendaya is not the stereotypical gym bunny, road-running or iron-pumping Hollywood star you'll find doing weights in the gym at 6 a.m. every day. Obviously, she exercises, but it's refreshing – not to mention encouraging – to learn that she does so on her own terms. But then, being Zendaya, she would, wouldn't she? That said, she does have certain genetic advantages which enable her to stay in such great shape. Hollywood still puts a lot of pressure on its leading ladies to look a certain way and, luckily for Zendaya, she has a fast metabolism that allows her to meet these exacting, if outdated, standards without extreme dieting or exercise regimes.

Having played a lot of sports growing up that included football (or as she would call it, soccer), running and basketball,

Zendaya has always had an active lifestyle. This continued when she gave up sports in favour of dance as a child. And it is dance that continues to form the bedrock of her exercise regime today.

'For me, I enjoy dancing and doing choreography, stuff like that. So, that's how I get my exercise,' she told *Justine* magazine. 'The priority is to find something that's really fun for you – whether that's jazzercise or whatever.'

When she's not working – which to be honest isn't that often – she'll take a dance class or dance at home, alone or with her assistant Darnell. She likes to have a dancing session almost every day, and some days her dance routine goes on for an hour or more. Like all of us, Zendaya knows that if she's not having fun, she won't enjoy her workout and therefore be less inclined to do one. So, she stays away from the gym and generic routines, being inclined instead to train and work out in preparation for television and films roles – such as when she learned to fly on trapeze for *The Greatest Showman.* She has also been known to channel her acting talents into working out, putting on a variety of wigs and pretending to be different people as she puts herself through the paces! She much prefers practising simple sweat sessions that can be done at home with little or no equipment to working out in the gym. Laid-back, that's her style. She has no set work-out routine, but she squeezes in circuit training sets at her home studio and in her back yard when she can. From plank variations using a medicine ball to dynamic stretching, sit-ups and arm raises, she moves straight from one exercise on to the next with minimal rest in-between sets to keep her energy levels high. One of her brothers, Austin, who is a personal trainer, writes her a programme and often puts her through her paces.

In addition to doing circuits, Zendaya loves to exercise by hiking in the hills close to her Hollywood home. Walking is one of the best forms of low-intensity steady-state cardio (LISS, a slower aerobic activity done for an extended period of time). It is great for boosting heart health without putting strain on the joints and provides benefits to mental health and sleep. Zendaya regularly shares images of her hikes, usually taken with Noon in tow, on social media. When he gets tired, she carries him on her back which gives an extra 'woof' to her workout and an extra 'aah' factor to comments from her followers.

Zendaya is just not a one workout kinda gal, preferring to mix it up with bouts of boxercise, plyometrics (jump training) and high-intensity aerobics. She has also practised Pilates and tries to fit in three quick sessions of full body yoga every week to target all her muscles while helping her stay toned and flexible. She may not have a regular exercise routine but it works. It's the Zendaya philosophy of life made physical. Find out what suits you and if you have fun, you'll keep on incorporating it into your life!

When it comes to her mental health, Zendaya is refreshingly upfront about the fact that she gets therapy. 'Of course, I go to therapy,' she told *Vogue*. 'I mean, if anybody is able to possess the financial means to go to therapy, I would recommend they do that. I think it's a beautiful thing. There's nothing wrong with working on yourself and dealing with those things with someone who can help you, someone who can talk to you, who's not your mom or whatever, who has no bias.'

She felt particularly under pressure when *Euphoria* was launched in June 2019. 'Although it was amazing and exciting, it was also extremely stressful. It gave me a lot of anxiety every week,' she revealed in an interview with *Elle* magazine. 'That's something I deal with – I have anxiety. I already know after this interview is over, I'm going to spiral about it for weeks.'

She blames the perfectionist, uber-Virgoan part of her for being too hard on herself at times. For piling the pressure on as she's constantly striving to do her best and not mess up. And that's when she finds it most beneficial to play her favourite music and just dance, dance, dance.

EIGHT

'Tomdaya'

'Happiest of birthdays to the one
who makes me the happiest' –
**Zendaya's message to Tom Holland
on his twenty-sixth birthday**

Only Zendaya and Tom Holland can know when the nature of their relationship changed from close friendship to deep love. There had, of course, been a connection as soon as they met, an alchemy at work which translated beautifully onto the big screen as they played out their roles as MJ Watson and Peter 'Spidey' Parker in the *Spider-Man* films. The rumour mill and the internet immediately went into overdrive, with much speculation regarding a romance between the pair. More than once, both Zendaya and Tom had denied these claims. 'We are friends,' Zendaya told *Variety* in 2017, 'He's a great dude.' Two years later, Tom insisted to *Elle* magazine that he was single. Still, the rumours persisted, but when Zendaya was spotted on holiday in Greece with her *Euphoria* co-star Jacob Elordi in 2019 – and was then seen kissing him in New York – these finally quietened down.

Heading into lockdown, it seemed that Tom was coupled up, too. It looked like he was dating English actress Nadia Parkes, of *The Spanish Princess* fame. It's believed the relationship started in February 2020, although news didn't leak out until the following summer, when the intensely private Holland posted a picture of her on Instagram. According to the *Daily Mail*, Nadia spent lockdown with Tom, Tom's brother and another friend at the Holland brothers' London flat. 'They made the decision to isolate together,' reported a source. 'Things have been going great between them. Tom has told friends and family they're in an official relationship and living together so soon into their romance has only made them stronger.'

However, by the time Zendaya and Tom reunited in Atlanta to shoot *Spider-Man: No Way Home in* October 2020, to all intents and purposes, both were single, with Holland thought to have broken up with Parkes shortly before the film started shooting. The pandemic continued to dominate proceedings, with the production reportedly relying on innovative new technology that scanned actors into a visual effects system that could apply make-up and costumes during post-production. A light system was also in place to signal when the cast could take off their masks for filming and when masks would be required while set work was undertaken. It's possible that lockdown made both Zendaya and Tom, like many other people during that strange time, realize what was really important in life. They were great friends already, so upon being reunited, one can only presume that their on-screen romance finally morphed into an off-screen one, too. They managed to keep their blossoming relationship a secret until 1 July 2021 when they were spotted – and photographed – in Holland's car while stationary at a red light in Los Angeles. They were also seen later that day in the Silver Lake neighbourhood of LA with Zendaya's mother, Claire. Social media went into meltdown. Not only was Zendaya trending worldwide on Twitter, but 'Tom Holland', 'Peter' and #SpiderManNoWayHome were listed as trending topics as well. 'F**KING FINALLY. TOM HOLLAND AND ZENDAYA ARE OFFICIALLY TOGETHER' one excited user tweeted. Another added, 'THIS IS NOT A DRILL. I REPEAT THIS IS NOT A DRILL.'

Neither Zendaya nor Tom denied the romance as they had in the past. In fact, as time went on, they were photographed together more and more, with Holland's social media posts to Zendaya becoming increasingly intimate. In honour of Zendaya's twenty-fifth birthday, Tom shared a mirror selfie of the alleged couple on the *Spider-Man* set on Instagram. In the caption he wrote, 'My MJ, have the happiest of birthdays. Gimme a call when your [*sic*] up xxx.' The 'My' wording caused yet another meltdown on social media with fans and followers delirious at the loved-up content. There were more posts in which he commented on Zendaya's beauty, making full use of flame and heart emojis. Without naming Zendaya, Tom spoke about their relationship to *GQ* magazine in November 2021.

'One of the downsides of our fame is that privacy isn't really in our control anymore, and a moment that you think is between two people that love each other very much is now a moment that is shared with the entire world,' he said.

He went on to say that he had decided to always keep his private life private because he shared so much of his life with the world as it was. 'We sort of felt robbed of our privacy,' he said, again omitting to name Zendaya. 'I don't think it's about not being ready – it's just that we didn't want to. You know, I respect her too much to say … this isn't my story. It's our story. And we'll talk about what it is when we're ready to talk about it together.'

Zendaya would refrain from publicly referring to Tom as her boyfriend for another ten months, by which time the whole world knew they were an item and had fallen madly in love with Zendaya and Tom – or, as they were being referred to, 'Tomdaya'. They were the cutest couple in showbiz, with the slow-burn element to their romance and the fact that they'd been such great friends to begin with suggesting that this was a relationship that had very un-Hollywood legs. It was cute and wholesome. *They* were cute and wholesome – and they still are.

A look into their respective backgrounds and it becomes increasingly clear why they are so well matched. Like Zendaya, Tom started his career early. A keen dancer as a kid who loved grooving along to Janet Jackson tracks at home, his mother sent him to dance class and then, aged nine, he began dancing at a hip-hop class close to his home in a leafy suburb of southwest London. While performing with his school at a local festival in 2006, he was spotted by an associate of the *Billy Elliot the Musical* choreographer. An audition was arranged, with the musical's director noting that he 'had great potential and was a very natural actor'. After two years of training in ballet, tap dancing and acrobatics, Holland won the role of Michael Caffrey, Billy's best friend, and made his debut performance in the West End in June 2008, when he was just twelve. He also started to learn gymnastics. Later that year, he was promoted to the title role in the musical. On his first day playing Billy Elliot, Holland developed tonsillitis, but he nevertheless performed onstage to positive reviews, demonstrating that he was a real trooper, just like his future Spidey co-star and girlfriend, Zendaya.

After his work on *Billy Elliot the Musical* finished in 2010, Holland voiced a role in the British dub of the Japanese animated fantasy film *The Secret World of Arrietty*. He sent an audition tape to director J. A. Bayona for a part in *The Impossible*, the film about the devastating Indian Ocean earthquake and tsunami of 2004. Bayona arranged a meeting and, impressed with Tom's emotional delivery, cast him in the film. Working on *The Impossible* made Tom realize that he wanted to pursue an acting career permanently. Holland received critical praise for his performance, winning several prestigious awards. He went on to appear in *How I Live Now* (2013), was a voice actor in *Locke* (2013) and featured in the film version of *Billy Elliot the Musical* (2014).

In 2015, he played Gregory Cromwell, son of Thomas, in the acclaimed television adaptation of Hilary Mantel's *Wolf Hall*. He also portrayed a second real-life historical character in the Ron Howard film *In the Heart of the Sea*, playing the young Thomas Nickerson (the famous nineteenth-century sailor and author who, at fourteen years old, had miraculously survived the whaleship *Essex* going down in the Pacific Ocean after it had been rammed by whale). Later in the year, he directed a short film in which a young man constructs a birdhouse with his beloved grandfather. This seemed to whet his appetite to direct, and he was to later say that he had ambitions to direct a full-length movie – rather like his future girlfriend. However, 2015 was mostly memorable for him landing the role that would change his life. Shortly before his nineteenth birthday, he signed a deal with Marvel Studios to play the teenage Peter Parker in a new raft of *Spider-Man* films. This really was a childhood dream come true for Holland. As a kid, he had been a huge fan of the comic-book hero – he had been the proud owner of thirty Spidey costumes in addition to matching bed sheets. He had to beat off tough competition to land the role, auditioning against 1,500 other teen actors from around the world. The film producers were said to be blown away by his dramatic skills, while the directors felt his dancing and gymnastics training and experience made him the perfect Spidey.

Until *Spider-Man*, Tom's career was UK-based. Hollywood was a whole different, and much bigger, much scarier ball game. He'd had a crush on Zendaya since seeing her on *Shake It Up*, and once he'd got over his mild case of 'star-struck-itis' on meeting her, he came to regard her as a source of showbiz wisdom. And once Zendaya realized what an awesome person and talent Tom was, she was more than happy to help guide him. She liked the fact that he was capable of outperforming her on occasion. His jaw-dropping, show-stopping performance of Rihanna's 'Umbrella' as part of *The Tonight Show*'s Lip Sync Battle in July 2017 was proof of that. He made her excellent, silk-pyjama-ed interpretation of Bruno Mars's hit '24K Magic' look tame in comparison. He told Zendaya it was his plan to outwork everyone as Spidey. She could relate to that – someone with a similar work ethic and drive to her own. They quickly formed their own mutual admiration society.

'Sometimes you just have to be a person to vent to, someone to just be there and listen … I was lucky enough where my life didn't change overnight,' Zendaya later told the Associated Press. 'I started when I was young, so it was kind of like a slow progression. I kind of got to learn it as I went and figure it out and get my footing a little bit, whereas for him it was so much all at once. I have an extreme amount of empathy for that, so anything that I learned or have learned or continue to learn, I share with him, and anything he learns he shares with me.'

Tom was equally complimentary, commenting that Zendaya was a wonderful companion, a 'wise old owl' teacher and a shoulder to cry on as they journeyed on the *Spider-Man* juggernaut together. As a boyfriend, he was loving and caring and never stopped telling Zendaya how beautiful she was. Publicly, too. In December 2021, he halted a red-carpet interview mid-flow at the premiere of *Spider-Man: No Way*

Home in order to gaze at her in total adoration as she arrived at the event in a fabulous spiderweb gown. Then there were his increasingly heartfelt Instagram posts. This is just what Zendaya had longed for. In a 2017 chat with assistant Darnell on her now-defunct app, which she originally set up in 2016 to allow fans to have a window into her world, she'd pondered on what she looked for in a boyfriend. 'Some people don't necessarily like the, "Oh you're beautiful, you're this, you're that,"' she said. 'Some people are like, "That's too much for me. I don't need to hear it all the time." Some people don't like it, it makes them uncomfortable. Me? I need you to vocalize that. I need to know, I need to hear it and I need to hear it often.'

However, their connection runs deeper than this. They have similar values. As with Zendaya, at the centre of Tom's world is his family – his parents, Dominic and Nicola, and three younger brothers, Harry, Sam and Paddy, are his bedrock. Like Zendaya, he enjoyed a secure and loving upbringing and remains very close to them all. Neither set of parents pushed their offspring into a showbiz life or into being a child star. It was Zendaya and Tom who did all the running. These elements, combined with the fact that Tom also speaks out for good causes and has set up a trust in the UK to support charity work, has a gracious humility to him, is forever grateful for his lot in life and the gifts he's been blessed with, make him and Zendaya kindred spirits. Soulmates, if you will.

Last but not least, both adore their dogs. Zendaya is dog-mother to her Noon, of course, while Tom has his Tessa – his beloved blue Staffordshire terrier whom he often refers to as 'Angel'.

With her private life in a very good place, Zendaya turned her attention back to her career. With *Spider-Man: No Way Home* in the can by March 2021, Zendaya's next appearance on the red carpet was at the Oscars a month later. She was presenting from the ceremony and took the 'wow' crown in a searingly bright yellow strapless cut-out gown by Valentino. The midriff-baring number also had a thigh-high slit, revealing matching yellow Jimmy Choo platform shoes. She accessorized with $6 million of Bulgari jewels. As a global ambassador for both Valentino and Bulgari, she showed off both luxury brands beautifully. Much of 2021 was also taken up with shooting the greatly anticipated second season of *Euphoria*, where she got to dip 'a tiny toe tip' back into the music industry after singing vocals on two songs that would feature in the new season (she had collaborated with British rapper and singer Labrinth on the song 'All for Us' for *Euphoria*'s first season). She also found time to voice the character of Lola Bunny in *Space Jam: A New Legacy* which premiered that July. She had loved the first *Space Jam* movie since childhood and drew on her experiences with her family's love of basketball for the role.

August and September 2021 saw her reunited with Timothée Chalamet on the hectic press tour for *Dune*, which was due for release on 15 September, having been postponed twice due to the Covid-19 pandemic. In addition to talking all things *Dune*, the tour was like her own travelling fashion show runway. At the *Dune* photocall in London, Zendaya wore a bold Vivienne Westwood top composed of interwoven chains. She paired the statement look with a tan and white check skirt and Christian

Louboutin heels. For the post-screening cocktail reception, she went for a more laid-back look, twinning a floor-length, white Peter Do button-down top with high-waisted, slim black leather trousers. A glittering necklace from Bulgari complimented the ensemble. For the premiere itself, she channelled *Star Wars'* Princess Leia in a sculptural, off-white sequin gown from the Rick Owens Fall 2021 collection. She completed the outfit with striking purple make-up, Bulgari's Serpenti Viper double-coil bracelet, and diamond rings. At the premiere after party, she modelled a very 2021 string cut-out, semi-sheer dress which featured geometric peek-a-boo designs and her signature high-thigh slit from the Nensi Dojaka Spring/Summer 2022 collection. At the photocall in Paris, she wore a plum-coloured, classy two-piece – a long-sleeve cropped top and high-waisted, figure-hugging skirt featuring a feather bottom – by Maison Alaïa. For the photocall at the prestigious Venice Film Festival, she stepped out in Look 46 from Valentino's latest couture collection – a black satin blazer emblazoned with her name and a red emoji-like heart, over a white dress designed with a high slit and a belt of bubblegum pink ribbon. She accessorized with several Bulgari rings, including a canary diamond from the house's Magnifica collection. However, her evening look was judged by *Vogue* to be one of her all-time best – a bespoke Balmain dress in softest flesh-hued leather which was draped across her body to look like wet fabric. The bespoke garment was crafted using an exact model of Zendaya's body, just as the deep pink Tom Ford breastplate she'd worn at the 2020 Critics' Choice Awards had been. The Balmain was ultimate (albeit very glamorous)

Chani – the desert warrior she portrayed in *Dune*. Emeralds and diamonds by Bulgari completed the look.

Unusually, Zendaya did not make an appearance at the Met Gala, which had been postponed from its usual May date to September due to the pandemic. 'I will be on *Euphoria*,' Zendaya revealed to *Extra Magazine* during the Venice leg of her *Dune* press tour. 'I know that this is the first time people are gonna hear that I'm not going. My fans will be very upset with me. I will unfortunately not be able to attend because I will be working on *Euphoria*. I got my time off to come here and do this Venice experience, which has been really, really special.'

Euphoria aside, it would be a fashion-filled autumn for Zendaya. In October she was named an honouree for Women in Film (WIF) Honors. The annual benefit supports the WIF's educational and philanthropic programmes and is an advocacy for gender parity for women throughout the industry. For the event, Zendaya rocked up in a fresh-off-the-runway grey dress from the Loewe Spring/Summer 2022 collection. Unconventionally, the design featured a sizeable gold chest plate in the front, which added a warrior-like vibe to the look. Zendaya matched the gold of the plate with a pair of shiny gold Louboutin pumps. Also in October, the Council of Fashion Designers of America announced that she was to be the youngest ever recipient of their prestigious Fashion Icon Award. Previous winners included Lady Gaga, Naomi Campbell and Beyoncé. The honour, which the organization said 'recognizes her global impact on fashion,' was presented to her on 10 November by supermodel Iman, who praised Zendaya's style, fearless fashion sense and self-confidence on the red carpet and beyond, saying she had inspired a whole new generation of fashion lovers, including Iman's own daughter, Lexi, whom she had with late husband David Bowie. Zendaya, announced Iman, transcended any known definition of celebrity style. Zendaya wore a Vera Wang bright red two-piece – a tight, bandeau crop top paired with a peplum-style maxi skirt. She wore her hair in long plaits and a whopping 60 carats of Bulgari diamonds.

'It's such an honour to be here tonight, on this stage, accepting this award that has been received by some of the most awe-inspiring, indelible forces that have undoubtedly changed the fashion game forever and I hope to do a fraction of what they all have done,' she said during her acceptance speech. 'I am incredibly grateful.' She later posted on Instagram, 'Last night was an absolute dream come true, thank you to the @cfda, this moment meant the world to @luxurylaw and I'.

It was all things Spidey that dominated the run up to Christmas 2021. *Spider-Man: No Way Home* premiered at the Fox Village Theatre in Los Angeles on 13 December. It was yet another red-carpet triumph for Zendaya. She dazzled onlookers – and, as previously mentioned, Tom – with a floor-length, custom-made, beige Valentino dress embellished with sparkly black spiderwebs. The gown featured a plunging neckline, low back and her trademark thigh-high slit. She completed the look with a black lace domino mask, matching Louboutin stilettos, Bulgari jewellery and her hair in cornrows. Tom and Zendaya, along with co-star Jacob Batalon, spent the evening in tears, their arms wrapped around each other as they watched each other up on-screen. 'It was so special,' Zendaya told *TIME* magazine.

It's thought that 'Tomdaya' spent their first Christmas and New Year together at Zendaya's home in Los Angeles. Noon and Tessa are also believed to have been in residence. The second season of *Euphoria* premiered on 9 January 2022, and a month later, the series was renewed for a third season. In an interview with *Vogue Italia*, Zendaya revealed that she had originally been down to direct an episode in the second season, but she'd pulled out on realizing that she was acting in the same episode. Ever the perfectionist, she wanted to be able to give her first serious attempt at directing her all and have enough time to do it the right way. *Euphoria*, with help from its new streaming home on HBO Max, averaged 16.3 million viewers an episode in season two, making it the most-watched show on the channel for eighteen years. Reviews were patchy, but Zendaya's performance gleaned nothing but praise. 'Zendaya puts on another masterful performance as Rue,' wrote The Review Geek. 'Zendaya remains heart-breaking and magnificent as Rue – doomed to replay her nightmarish cycle of destructive behaviour, her reliance on whatever substances she can find as strong as it ever was,' reported *The Guardian*. For Zendaya herself, playing Rue continued to give her fulfilment, purpose and relevance as an actor.

'Sometimes I feel kind of silly being an actor,' she told *Vogue Italia*. 'Because it's like I make-believe for a living, which may seem ridiculous, but then I remember the stories that I'm telling and the reasons behind them. Especially as of recent with *Euphoria*. I had so many people reach out and share their experiences of connecting with it, in the sense of loss or addiction or grief or mental illness and their struggles with that.'

For the 2022 Oscars, Zendaya rocked a Valentino Haute Couture white cropped shirt and silver sequin embroidered evening skirt designed for her by creative director Pierpaolo Piccioli. She finished the look with Valentino Garavani shoes covered in crystals, and a bonanza of Bulgari bling at her throat and wrists. *People* magazine hailed it as a look that would top the Oscars all-time best dressed lists for years to come.

Next up was filming another movie: *Challengers*, a romantic sports-centric comedy, in which she plays a tennis player-turned-coach who transforms her husband from a mediocre player into a world-famous grand slam champion. To jolt him out of a losing streak, she makes him play a 'Challenger' event where he finds himself standing across the net from his former best friend, who also happens to be his wife's ex. The part required Zendaya to spend three months training with pro-tennis coach Brad Gilbert to get her proficient enough at the sport to look like a credible coach. She also acted as producer on the film. The subject matter was something of a departure for Zendaya, but when had she not welcomed becoming involved in something new? The film was shot in Boston, and Tom visited her in the city on several occasions.

In May 2022, Zendaya was named by *TIME* magazine as one of the most influential 100 people in the world, and she was one of just five of the 100 who was selected to grace their own cover. For the shoot, she wore a red ruffled dress by Valentino, designed by its creative director Pierpaolo Piccioli.

He was fulsome in his praise, calling her 'authentic, fragile, and strong at the same time and she is without any doubt the most powerful voice of a generation.'

Dune auteur Denis Villeneuve paid tribute to her within the pages of *TIME*: 'To me, Zendaya is a thousand years old,' he wrote. 'She has already lived many lives before this one. And yet, she is as young as springtime. By some inextricable paradox, she also gives the impression of having been born sometime far into the future. She is timeless, and she can do it all. In just the past year or so, Zendaya has radiated like a shooting star captured on celluloid in Sam Levinson's *Malcolm & Marie*. She emotionally exploded as her teenage years disintegrated in Levinson's cultural phenomenon *Euphoria*. She shone in *Spider-Man: No Way Home*, a movie that dominated the box office in a year when she became the muse of extremes. But Zendaya is much more than that. She is an autonomous creative force herself. A cultural icon in the making. A person driven by pure inspiration, empathy, and respect for her craft, who uses authenticity as a new superpower. She seems fearless, her roots run deep, and I love that she still laughs like a kid. Zendaya is the future. And there is nothing more comforting to me. This is only the beginning.'

Zendaya was humbled – by both the accolade from *TIME* and Denis's heartfelt statement. 'A great honour,' she posted on social media. 'Thank you *TIME* for this acknowledgment, and to Denis for his kind words. This means the world to me'.

Another honour came when she was nominated in a number of categories for the 2022 Emmys: Outstanding Lead Actress in a Drama Series and Outstanding Drama Series for her role as executive producer on *Euphoria*. She was also part of the nomination for Outstanding Original Music and Lyrics for the show's songs 'I'm Tired' and 'Elliot's Song', having sung and had input into both.

'I'm overwhelmed,' Zendaya told *Vanity Fair*. 'It's absolutely insane. *Euphoria* has been such a great learning ground for me. The show obviously means so much to me and so much to everyone who makes it. People put their absolute heart and soul into this, and I am so lucky to share this with all of them. I've already talked to so many people on FaceTime, and I have a lot more texts to send out. But I am so proud of our team and the work we do together. I'm very, very proud.'

The song nominations were the icing – and the cherry – on the cake. Zendaya felt these had been integral to the narrative, enhancing the emotional journey of the characters and telling their stories through a different medium.

Having spent her twenty-sixth birthday in New York City with Tom, Zendaya returned to Los Angeles for the seventy-fourth Emmys on 12 September. Wearing an elegant strapless and voluminous black Valentino gown with Bulgari gems twinkling away at her throat, Zendaya made history (again) when she took the award for Outstanding Lead Actress in a drama series. At twenty-six, she became the youngest two-time winner for acting in Emmys history, and the first Black woman to win the Emmy for lead actress in a drama series twice over. She began her acceptance speech by thanking HBO 'for making such a safe space for making this very difficult show' and creator Sam

Levinson 'for sharing Rue with me,' adding, 'Thank you for believing in me – even in moments when I didn't believe in myself.'

Zendaya's mother, Claire, was present at the ceremony and revealed on Instagram how she was almost stopped from approaching her daughter. In a caption, she wrote, '[I] made my way to Z before they awarded her the Emmy to give her the biggest hug and say... breathe!!! The man who tried to stop me said "Where are your credentials?" I said "I'm Zendaya's mom" and kept walking!! Hahaha! I never name drop like that but I have to do it!'

Zendaya shared a heart-warming moment with her fans after Tom had been unable to join her at the 2022 Emmys due to filming commitments. The two-time Emmy winner was asked by *E! News* for the identity of the first person she had contacted after her historic win.

'I didn't have to text my mom because my mom was already there,' Zendaya replied. 'She's here tonight, which is very special. And I text my boyfriend.' This was the first occasion where she openly referred to Tom as such, although she had alluded to their relationship when chatting to *GQ* magazine in late 2021 – specifically about being papped when they were enjoying time alone together.

'It was quite strange and weird and confusing and invasive,' she said. 'The equal sentiment [we both share] is just that when you really love and care about somebody, some moments or things, you wish were your own ... I think loving someone is a sacred thing and a special thing and something that you want to deal with and go through and experience and enjoy amongst the two people that love each other.' This, however, is one of the inevitable downsides to A-list fame.

October saw Tom join Zendaya in Paris, where she attended the Valentino Spring/Summer 2023 show at Paris Fashion Week. In a city teeming with A-listers and top models, she had stolen the show in a completely sheer Valentino bodysuit with matching sequinned shorts and an oversized blazer, topping off the look with a pair of black chandelier earrings. The next day, she dressed down somewhat, wearing a comfortable but still chic blue shirt dress with the sleeves rolled up as she and Tom walked, hand-in-hand, around the world-famous Louvre Museum.

The main photography for *Dune: Part Two* commenced in November 2022, although Zendaya had done some filming on the production in Hungary a few months earlier. She jetted out to the UAE on location and shared a shot on her Instagram stories of a stunning sunset from the desert with the words, 'I know I've been quiet, but I'm here, just working as usual ... sending love from Arrakis.'

Zendaya's role as Chani, the desert warrior and protagonist Paul Atreides' love interest, would figure far more in the sequel and she was excited by the prospect – as was her co-star, Timothée Chalamet. 'It's amazing,' he told *Variety*. 'She's bringing exactly what she brought to the first one – which was incredible – but in greater abundance. And she's really become a sister. I'm so grateful to count her as a partner [in the film] and a sister and a friend.'

If Zendaya had written a dream career plan when starting out, it surely couldn't have been better than this – the one she was living.

The Complete 'Tomdaya' Timeline

A date-by-date account of how close friendship became true love.

7 July 2016: Tom refers to Zendaya as his 'friend'

Tom spoke about his relationship with Zendaya to *People*, referring to her as his friend. 'We are like the best of friends. She's so great and amazing,' he said. 'Zendaya is super famous and she's been through this and I just call her up and say, "How do I manage being famous?" I'm very glad I have a friend like her.'

10 July 2016: Tom Holland and Zendaya post about each other on Instagram

Soon after Zendaya and Tom were cast in *Spider-Man: Homecoming*, the pair started popping up in each other's Instagrams. Tom posted a photo of him and Zendaya in the pool with a friend with the caption 'Summer Sundays'.

9 November 2016: Zendaya shares her and Tom's photo on The Hollywood Reporter cover

Zendaya shared a photo of herself and Tom on the cover of *The Hollywood Reporter*, referring to her *Spider-Man* co-star as 'the very best'.

13 July 2017: rumours appear that Tom and Zendaya are dating

A source tells *People* magazine that they started seeing each other while filming *Spider-Man: Homecoming*, saying that the pair were being careful to keep their blossoming relationship private. It was mooted that they'd taken a holiday together – but it seems this was the publicity tour for the film.

8 August 2017: Zendaya denies relationship rumours

Zendaya spoke to *Variety* about her friendship with Tom, once again denying a relationship. 'We are friends,' she reiterated. 'He's literally one of my best friends and this past how many months, we've had to do press tours together.'

8 May 2018: Tom is awestruck by Zendaya's Met Gala look

She channelled Joan of Arc in a sparkling silver armour-inspired Versace dress, complete with a thigh-high slit and multiple cut-outs. 'All hail the queen,' he wrote on Instagram. 'Killing it, mate 🙌.'

30 August 2019: it's rumoured Zendaya is dating her *Euphoria* co-star Jacob Elordi

They're seen holidaying together in Greece and are later photographed kissing in New York City.

February 2020: Tom reportedly starts dating actress Nadia Parkes

However, news of their relationship doesn't emerge until around July 2020 when Tom posts a picture of Nadia on Instagram. They're said to have moved into together during lockdown.

September 2020: Zendaya and Jacob Elordi have split – if they ever were a proper couple

Jason is seen having dinner in Malibu with his now girlfriend, Kaia Gerber, on 1 September, Zendaya's twenty-fourth birthday.

30 June 2021: Zendaya and Tom are seen having dinner in Los Angeles

1 July 2021: Zendaya and Tom are papped kissing!

They are spotted in Tom's car while stopped at a red light in Los Angeles – this must certainly mean they're together after all!

9 July 2021: Zendaya talks about working with Tom over the past five years

In an interview with E! News, she says 'It's pretty special to have grown up together'.

13 December 2021: the LA premiere for *Spider-Man: No Way Home*

Tom calls a halt to his red-carpet interview so he can watch the arrival of Zendaya, who looks sensational in a custom-made spiderweb dress.

15 December 2021: Zendaya sends Tom loved-up message on Instagram

It's a childhood shot of him in one of his Spider-Man costumes and also a snap from the latest film. 'My Spider-Man,' she posts, complete with heart emoji.

16 December 2021: a *Spider-Man* press junket

Tom and Zendaya joke about him appearing in an episode of *Euphoria*, with Tom revealing that he's visited her on-set at least thirty times.

17 February 2022: Tom and Zendaya hang out in New York City

They enjoy dinner together and a screening of Tom's new film, *Uncharted*. At a New York Rangers ice hockey game, they're seen wearing matching Rangers jerseys with the other's name on them.

24 February 2022: Tom surprises Zendaya in Italy

She's working in Rome as the face of Valentino's latest campaign.

26 April 2022: Zendaya and Tom hit the stores in Boston

As Zendaya films the movie *The Challengers* in Boston, she and Tom are seen shopping in the city, with Elle reporting they visited Rolex and Cartier.

1 June 2022: Zendaya posts a romantic message on Insta for Tom's twenty-sixth birthday

A black and white snap of the pair in each other's arms appears on Instagram with Zendaya's caption, 'Happiest of birthdays to the one who makes me the happiest'.

8 June 2022: the internet refers to Tom as 'Mr. Zendaya'

27 August 2022: Tom and Zendaya get cosy in Budapest

While Zendaya is in Budapest in Hungary to film the *Dune* sequel, it looks like long distance is no match for our favourite *Spider-Man* couple. Tom flies all the way across the pond to visit his girlfriend.

1 September 2022: Zendaya's twenty-sixth birthday

Entertainment Tonight reports on Zendaya enjoying a low-key dinner with Tom, her mother, Claire, and *Euphoria* co-star Hunter Schafer in New York City as she celebrates her birthday.

12 September 2022: the Emmys

Looking stunning in a black Valentino gown, Zendaya wins an Emmy – her second – for playing Rue in *Euphoria*. Tom is not in attendance, but Zendaya tells *E! News* that he – 'her boyfriend' – is the first person she texted after her win.

8 October 2022: Paris Fashion Week

Zendaya and Tom are spotted holding hands as they visit the iconic Louvre Museum in the French capital.

25 February 2023: Tom drops three 😍 emojis

These emojis were in response to his girlfriend's appearance at the 2023 NAACP Image Awards. Zendaya arrives in an archival black and green Versace gown before changing into a white Prada Spring/Summer 1993 two-piece dress. The next day, on the 2023 SAG red carpet, she wears a pink Valentino gown adorned with 3D roses before changing into silky Giorgio Armani.

12 March 2023: in the UK

A relaxed-looking, make-up-free Zendaya joins Tom and his parents in Richmond Park, Surrey, to walk their dogs.

19 March 2023: Zendaya wears Tom's ring!

Getting a manicure in London, Zendaya is spotted wearing a gold signet ring engraved with Tom's initials on her middle finger.

Late March 2023: in Mumbai, India

Before attending an official function, the couple are seen on the Instagram page of the yacht chartering service Blue Bay Marine as they enjoy time out on the ocean.

2 April 2023: Zendaya and Tom photographed while leaving Mumbai

Although the pair decided to go solo on the NMACC red carpet in Mumbai and steered clear of any public displays of affection, pap shots show Tom and Zendaya the following day walking hand-in-hand as they're leaving their hotel for the airport.

16 May 2023: 'Tomdaya' photographed on holiday in Venice, Italy

The couple are snapped packing on the PDA (public display of affection) on a romantic gondola ride.

1 June 2023: Tom's twenty-seventh birthday

Zendaya posts two never-seen-before photos of him on her Instagram stories, captioned with plenty of heart emojis.

NINE

What the Future Holds

'I always say my idol is my future
self. I don't know who she is yet, I
haven't met her yet, but I know she's
there and she's waiting for me in the
future.' – **Zendaya, *Women's Wear Daily***

New Year 2023 could hardly have begun more auspiciously for
Zendaya. On 11 January, she won the Golden Globe for Best
Actress in a television series for *Euphoria*, yet, unusually for
this queen of the red carpet, she failed to attend the ceremony.
Work commitments were cited, although it was later revealed

that she had actually been in Los Angeles on the night the event was taking place. The internet was abuzz, suggesting that she was deliberately snubbing the Awards because her previous two Golden Globe nominations – for playing Rue in *Euphoria* in 2020 and a year later for her performance in *Malcolm & Marie,* respectively – had failed to bring home the much-coveted trophy. However, Zendaya's official acceptance speech – sent via her Instagram page – was as gracious and humble as ever.

'I'm so sorry I wasn't able to be there tonight, but I just wanted to say thank you to @goldenglobes for this incredible honor,' she wrote alongside a photo of herself on-set as Rue. 'To my fellow nominees, it is a privilege to be named beside you, I admire you all deeply. Thank you to my *Euphoria* family, without you, none of this is possible. Lastly, thank you from the bottom of my heart to everyone who has allowed Rue into theirs. I think everyone knows how much she means to me, but the fact that she can mean something to someone else is a gift. I'm honestly at a loss for words as I type this, all I can say is thank you, thank you, thank you. Goodnight.'

Four days later, she nabbed the trophy for playing Rue at the Critics' Choice Awards in the Best Actress in a Drama Series category but missed this ceremony, too. Again, existing work commitments were given as the reason for her no-show. Again, she took to Instagram to express her thanks at the victory, accompanied by a black and white photo of herself on a bicycle.

'Woke up to some incredible news... thank you so much @criticschoice for this honor,' read her caption. 'I can't stop smiling and can't express how grateful I am.'

It wasn't until 25 February that she made her 2023 red carpet debut at the NAACP Image Awards, where she wowed onlookers and fashionistas alike even more than usual by orchestrating a quick change halfway through the evening. Initially walking the red carpet in a strapless black and green, figure-skimming vintage Versace dress that featured a plunging neckline and high-thigh slits, she then slid into her own take on a Prada Spring/Summer 1993 look, consisting of a bralette featuring cut-out stars and a matching skirt with cut-out stars in the waistband, styled with toweringly high-heeled white pumps. She was also present at the Screen Actors Guild Awards two days later, having been nominated for Outstanding Performance by a Female Actor in a Drama Series for playing Rue. She looked particularly pretty-in-pink on the red carpet in a strapless, blush pink, figure-hugging Valentino gown with a train covered in sculpted, life-sized rosettes. The dress featured a tight-fitting bodice and a trumpet silhouette with a train. She completed the look with Bulgari jewels: a diamond choker necklace with green, orange and purple gems, as well as a diamond cuff bracelet. Zendaya lost out to *The White Lotus*'s Jennifer Coolidge, but she didn't appear to let this faze her. She took to the stage to present an award with *Normal People* actor Paul Mescal – after having changed into a slinky, strapless Giorgio Armani Privé gown that featured a sequined black bustier, pale pink and baby blue diagonal sections, and a statement cut-out panel underneath the bust. Her two sublimely sartorial selections apart, there was speculation on social media that she had deliberately snubbed Mescal as they both made their way to the stage and he attempted to take her hand. The most likely explanation, however, was that it had been a simple miscommunication, with Zendaya holding out her elbow in an attempt to link arms, rather than deliberately rebuffing him.

Early March saw Zendaya across the pond in Paris for Paris Fashion Week, for the Autumn/Winter 2023 collections. She made a surprise appearance at the Louis Vuitton show, hosted at the Musée d'Orsay, wearing head-to-toe LV tiger print. The ensemble included a matching striped suit jacket (which she wore open), short shorts and knee-high boots paired with a black micro bikini top and a mini monogrammed Louis Vuitton handbag and co-ordinating gold jewellery. Causing major traffic upheaval, hundreds of fans and onlookers lined the street outside the venue to witness her arrival along with fellow A-listers Emma Stone, Ana de Armas, Alicia Vikander, and the newly appointed Louis Vuitton Men's Creative Director, Pharrell Williams. Zendaya and Law Roach snuck in just as the lights were about to go down. As previously mentioned, there was some drama surrounding Zendaya and Law's seating at the fashion show. While Zendaya sat on the highly coveted front row between Emma Stone and Dior CEO Delphine Arnault, Law appeared to be seatless until a space was hurriedly found for him elsewhere. After the show, Zendaya joked that on the way to the show she should have ridden a bicycle rather than taken a car as it would have been quicker. She then happily posed for photos with fans, unaware of the bomb Law was about to drop. One might presume that he would have informed her of his plans to retire from celebrity styling, but it appears he did not.

After the shock announcement, Zendaya called Law in disbelief. 'She said, "Girl, I thought we make big decisions together",' Law revealed on model Emily Ratajkowski's podcast, *High Low with Emrata*, shortly after he announced his retirement. He went on to reveal that she'd added, 'Do you need me to send you on a vacation? Like tell me what you're going through.' Law said that he told her how unhappy he was, how he'd been feeling low for some time and was still grieving the death of his nephew who had tragically passed away, aged just three years old, in November 2021. Law had said at the time, in a since-deleted Instagram post, that it was the toughest thing he had ever had to deal with. As Law poured out his heart and soul, Zendaya listened to him with great love and sympathy before telling him, 'Whatever you need, whatever you need.' However, there was no way that Law was ever going to abandon his 'little sister', even though she was now all grown up. Hadn't they made a solemn vow at the start of their relationship back in 2011 to do everything they possibly could to elevate each other? They'd dubbed themselves, 'Big ideas, Small detail.' Law was the big ideas person who lived in a fantasy world, sourcing the most gorgeous and unusual garments for Zendaya to wear, which she would pull together to wow on the red carpet. Then Law would create the narrative behind the look, telling her what the story was and revealing the identity of this goddess strutting her stuff. And Zendaya would then become that character.

They had been a team for so long: it was Law's genius that had played such a major role in enabling her to transform from cute but ordinary Disney kid to the superstar she had become by 2023. How would she manage if Law was no longer at her side at these pivotal moments and, indeed, during the detailed planning stages that always came beforehand? But it seems he never intended not to be. Less than a month later, on 1 April, Law was at Zendaya's side, actually on the red carpet with her, at the opening of the Nita Mukesh Ambani Cultural Centre in Mumbai, India. And they wore co-ordinating outfits no less. Zendaya walked the red carpet in a midnight blue sari-inspired design with sparkling embellishments and a trailing train. Underneath, she wore a gold bralette with leaf-shaped sequins. Meanwhile, Law wore a two-piece floor-length black gown covered in stunning floral embroidery. Both pieces were created by Indian designer Rahul Mishra, whose exquisite designs Zendaya had worn once before at a Bulgari launch in 2022. On her arrival back in Los Angeles, she shared a post on her Instagram profile, in which she summed up her experience in Mumbai: 'I had the most extraordinary night celebrating NMACC India. Thank you, Mumbai for the warmest and kindest welcome. And to Rahul Mishra for your beautiful creations, it was an honor for Law Roach and I to wear your work yet again.'

It was possibly due to Law's presence in Mumbai that she and Tom, who was also at the gala, chose not to be photographed together as a couple. There was speculation on social media that their lack of togetherness signified that all was not well in Tomdaya-land, but this was swiftly squashed when they were snapped hand-in-hand as they left for the airport.

Prior to the India trip, Tomdaya had skipped the Oscars in March in favour of spending a little family time chez Holland in the

UK, where the loved-up pair were photographed while enjoying some very un-star-like activities, such as walking the dogs with Mr and Mrs Holland and supermarket shopping. Zendaya, dressed down and make-up free, proved her down-to-earth credentials by happily standing aside when Tom was asked for a selfie by a young Spidey fan outside a shop. There was no 'hey, what about me?' diva-type hissy fit from her. In fact, she held her boyfriend's jacket while he was being snapped. A few days later, while she was having a manicure in a local beauty salon, her nail technician noticed she was wearing a ring bearing Tom's initials. The tech took a snap of Zendaya's nails and posted it on Instagram, resulting in yet another social media meltdown. The couple also sneaked in a date at historic Hampton Court Palace – King Henry VIII's favourite palace – where they were treated to an after-hours tour with historian and author Tracy Borman. 'I've had some special moments at the Hampton Court Palace,' Borman tweeted shortly after the visit, 'but this has to count as one of the best ever: exploring Hampton Court after hours with @TomHolland1996 [and] @Zendaya.' Borman shared a picture of herself with the couple plus another romantic image, showing Tom and Zendaya's silhouettes side-by-side on a rooftop, with their heads leaning against each other.

As 2023 progresses, Zendaya's diary is predictably full. Highlights include collecting the NATO Spirit of the Industry Award and the Comedy Ensemble of the Year Award in Las Vegas at the end of April, the release of sports rom-com *Challengers* in September and the release of *Dune: Part Two* in November. A fourth Spidey film starring Tom and Zendaya is also in development. 'All I will say is that we have the story,' Marvel president Kevin Feige revealed in a February 2023 interview with *Entertainment Weekly*. 'We have big ideas for that and our writers are just putting pen to paper now.' There's also a third series of *Euphoria*, but it's unlikely that season three will start shooting before the latter half of 2023, which realistically means the new season won't premiere before mid-2024. Whenever filming commences, Zendaya will try to ensure that, this season, she finally gets behind the camera to fulfil her ambition to direct an episode – and maybe more than just one. She's been learning the craft from *Euphoria*'s director of photography, Marcell Rév.

'Anyone who's seen his work can attest to the fact that he's a master of his craft,' she told *Interview* magazine. 'When I'm on set, I'll ask him what all the names of the different lights are and what they do and why they need them, and I try to guess what he's going to say before he says it. I'm always so nervous to try things because I don't want to not be great at them.'

The thought of directing certainly excites, inspires and stimulates her. It's the reason she spends so much time on-set, even when scenes she's not a part of are being shot. The whole experience is a learning curve for her. She soaks up information up like a sponge and takes it all in. As well as Marcell, she's constantly talking to other crew members, wanting to know what they're doing and why, and asking them to explain technical terms and procedures to her. The aim is that one day she will be able to make what she wants to see – the scenes, the films, the television shows.

In the early days of working on *Euphoria*, Sam Levinson, the drama series creator, predicted that Zendaya will direct and is in no doubt it will happen. Not just on *Euphoria* but also other future projects and productions. 'In watching her act and just talking to her about film, you just realize, very quickly, that this is someone who has no ceiling to their talent,' Levinson shared about Zendaya. 'She finishes an emotionally insane day, does beautiful work, and then is just chilling and talking to our gaffer or about the lighting, or whatever. I'm just looking at her and I'm like, "Oh, it's gonna be a year or two before she's directing". She's so meticulous and so thoughtful about it. It's inspiring, as a storyteller and as someone who's able to push the show wherever it wants to go. It just really excites me.'

Zendaya's role as Rue has seen her break records and make history as an actress. The youngest woman to ever win an Emmy for Best Actress in a Drama Series in 2020, and as the only Black – and youngest – woman to win two Emmys in this category in 2022. But according to Puck News, 2023 has also been a record-breaking year for her when it comes to *Euphoria*. The showbiz website claims she has negotiated a new deal with HBO that will make her one of the highest-paid television actors in Hollywood, and maybe one of the youngest to land such a deal. It's thought, that as both star and co-producer, she will be earning close to $1 million per episode. If true, she will be joining the ranks of the other one million dollars-per-ep fraternity. These include the lead cast of *Friends* in their final season, the lead cast of *Game of Thrones*, Nicole Kidman and Reese Witherspoon for *Big Little Lies*, and Elisabeth Moss on Apple's *Shining Girls*. Zendaya hitting the one million mark possibly makes her the youngest, highest-paid Black female actor on television. Ever.

Looking forward as we approach the mid-2020s, there is still much Zendaya wishes to achieve in her already stellar career. 'Other than becoming a director, my dream is to create my own things,' she told *InStyle* magazine. 'I would love to make films that allow space for young up-and-coming artists, writers, and filmmakers – because especially with black talent, it's not a lack thereof; it's a lack of opportunity. I'd like to give those opportunities: Partner upcoming filmmakers with different writers and mentorships, connect them with the actors they want to see in their films, and create those special bonds. And make sure they get paid and taken care of.'

One particular story she wishes to tell is a tale about two Black girls who fall in love. She told her friend and *Euphoria* co-star Colman Domingo in a chat with *Interview* magazine that she wanted such a scenario to be rooted in a beautiful and simple narrative about two people falling for each other. Something that would leave viewers feeling happy and falling in love with themselves. She added that while she was quite the romantic, she had never seen a similar story without it dealing more with the traumatic side of life. It was very important to talk about that, true, but she also loved the idea of a coming-of-age story where awkward and funny things happened, just like in real life when young people are trying to work out the complexities of relationships and who they are.

'Our existence is broad and expansive and beautiful, and to see all the different emotional colors of what it means to be a young Black girl,' she revealed to Colman. 'I would like to see that, because I don't think I've seen many depictions of it.'

She wants to make art that reflects life.

'Hopefully my ability to be a storyteller, to make those stories that I haven't seen, to showcase different forms of Black love and the different colours of our emotional experience – that will be my speaking out,' she revealed to *Interview* magazine in 2021.

She longs to relate stories and life experiences that have not yet been seen and translate them to film. She has always felt that we learn how to be human beings not just by interactions with each other but by watching films and television. Identifying with characters and seeing versions of ourselves – or rather the people we'd like to be – on-screen. She knows what it's like to want to be a favourite television character (Hannah Montana, in her case). So many people, she has said, have built the personas that they take out into the world based on what they've seen in films and on television.

Moving forward, it's thought that Zendaya has another big acting project on the horizon. According to several reports, she is in talks to play the late Ronnie Spector, lead singer of the Ronettes, in an upcoming biopic. A production company has secured Ronnie's life rights for the film, as well as the rights to her autobiography, *Be My Baby*. It's thought Pulitzer-winning playwright Jackie Sibblies Drury is in consideration to write the script. The biopic will focus on how the Ronettes were formed and eventually signed to Philles Records, the record company run by Phil Spector, who would, of course, later become

Ronnie's husband. The group recorded their hit 'Be My Baby' at the label. According to *Variety*, the film will also cover the Spectors' acrimonious divorce in 1974 and Ronnie's battle to win back the rights to her music. While there are several other singing and dancing actresses out there who no doubt could 'be Ronnie' to a satisfactory standard, Zendaya is in a class of her own when it comes to 'triple threat' talent. And as a hard-to-beat bonus, she is the chosen one: Ronnie Spector herself, *Variety* has reported, personally selected Zendaya to play her before she passed away in January 2022. According to Deadline, it is similar to the scenario of Aretha Franklin choosing Jennifer Hudson to play her in the biopic *Respect* before the 'Queen of Soul' passed away in 2018. Before Ronnie's death, it is believed that she herself was a producer on the production along with her manager Jonathan Greenfield, Marc Platt of *The Little Mermaid* and *Dear Evan Hansen* fame, and ... Zendaya.

Following Ronnie's death, Zendaya wrote a moving note commemorating Spector's life and her blossoming friendship with the musician: 'This news just breaks my heart. To speak about her as if she's not with us feels strange as she is so incredibly full of life. There's not a time I saw her without her iconic red lips and full teased hair, a true rockstar through and through. Ronnie, being able to know you has been one of the greatest honors of my life. Thank you for sharing your life with me, I could listen to your stories for hours and hours. Thank you for your unmeasured talent, your unwavering love for performing, your strength, resilience and your grace. There is absolutely nothing that could dim the light you cast.' She continued, 'I admire you so much and am so grateful for the bond we share. You are a magical force of greatness and the world of music will never be the same. I wish everyone got to experience you the way I did. We celebrate your beautiful life and give you all the flowers you so rightfully deserve. Rest in great power Ronnie. I hope to make you proud.'

When – and, indeed, if – the film ever gets made remains to be seen, but fans of both Ronnie and Zendaya are waiting with great anticipation. It should be the ultimate biopic, with Zendaya in a never-ending display of iconic sixties and seventies looks, utilizing her prodigious dancing talent for the first time since *Shake It Up,* singing those classic Ronette hits and using her *Euphoria*-honed acting skills. It must certainly be an Academy Award just waiting to be won.

A glance at Zendaya's long list of credentials, starting from the earliest days, would lead one to believe that she has masterminded her career from the start. While it's true to say she has always been ambitious, driven, focused and knew what she wanted, she maintains that there's never been a plan and that if she suddenly stops enjoying what she does, she would have no hesitation in walking away and doing something else.

'I don't necessarily have a plan. I've never really thought, "I have to do this by this time and I want to do this by that time,"' she told *Interview* magazine. 'I just want to do the things that make me happy and bring me joy and fulfil me as an artist, as a person. So, I keep that loose, because if one day it turns into a completely different career path, then I would allow myself to do that.'

Away from film and fashion and all things career-centric, what of Zendaya's future? With her worldly wisdom, empathy, innate intelligence and keen sense of justice, who would be surprised if one day she becomes the USA's first female president? Her popularity is boundless, with latest figures showing that her Instagram is followed by a simply mind-boggling 182 million people – and that number is growing all the time. There is also her personal future – what of Tom? In 2021, he gave an interview to *People* magazine in which he admitted he didn't feel it would be long before he started a family.

'I want to take a break and focus on starting a family and figuring out what I want to do outside of this world,' he said. 'I love kids. I can't wait to be a dad – I can wait, and I will, but I can't wait! If I'm at a wedding or a party, I'm always at the kids' table hanging out. My dad's been such a great role model for me. I think I've got that from him.'

Could Zendaya become the mother of those future children her boyfriend is so excited about welcoming into the world? The millions and millions of Tomdaya fans and followers are very much hoping so. Tom's newly renovated home in his native southwest London certainly looks large enough to house a growing family, but would Zendaya realistically be willing to relocate from her native California to raise a family in the UK? More to the point, although she's spoken of wanting children one day, is in love with the little girl who plays young Rue in *Euphoria*, and totally adores her young nieces and nephews, is she really ready to settle down with Tom and have kids of her own yet? It remains to be seen.

Zendaya has such a bright future, who knows what's in store? Will she continue her glittering career, perhaps with it being even more stellar than she's achieved thus far? Will she fulfil her ambition to direct a feature film? Will she continue to be a voice for her generation inspiring others to achieve their dreams? To be a much-revered role model? A spokesperson for people of colour? And will she have a happy marriage? A brood of adorable Tomdaya tots? Watch this space – if anyone can do it, it's Zendaya Maree Stoermer Coleman!

INDEX

PICTURE CREDITS

Page 1: Henri Szwarc / ABACAPRESS.com / Alamy (top); Mediapunch / Shutterstock (bottom)

Page 2: Billy Farrell / BFA / Shutterstock (top); Bill McCay / WireImage / Getty Images (bottom)

Page 3: Dan MacMedan / WireImage / Getty Images

Page 4: David Fisher / Shutterstock (top); Odette Martin / Shutterstock (bottom)

Page 5: David Fisher / Shutterstock

Page 6: HBO / Kobal / Shutterstock (top); Vicky Flores / EPA-EFE / Shutterstock (bottom)

Page 7: David Fisher / Shutterstock (top); Lumeimages / Shutterstock (bottom)

Page 8: Chelsea Lauren / Shutterstock (top); Laurent Zabulon / ABACAPRESS.com / Alamy (bottom)